HABITS OF THE HOUSEHOLD

SIMPLE PRACTICES TO HELP YOU AND
YOUR FAMILY DRAW CLOSER TO GOD

BIBLE STUDY GUIDE | FIVE SESSIONS

JUSTIN WHITMEL EARLEY

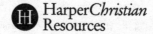
HarperChristian
Resources

Habits of the Household Bible Study Guide

© 2023 by Avodah, LLC

Requests for information should be addressed to:

Published in Grand Rapids, Michigan, by HarperChristian Resources. HarperChristian Resources is a registered trademark of HarperCollins Christian Publishing, Inc.

Requests for information should be addressed to customercare@harpercollins.com.

ISBN 978-0-310-17002-0 (softcover)
ISBN 978-0-310-17003-7 (ebook)

HarperChristian Resources titles may be purchased in bulk for church, business, fundraising, or ministry use. For information, please e-mail ResourceSpecialist@ChurchSource.com.

Published in association with Don Gates of the literary agency The Gates Group - www.thegates-group.com.

First Printing October 2023 / Printed in the United States of America

CONTENTS

A NOTE FROM JUSTIN

Habits are fascinating things. They are the everyday actions we do again and again, whether semiconsciously or unconsciously. They allow us to do complicated tasks on autopilot, like flipping pancakes or changing diapers while also chatting with a spouse about an issue or mulling over a work problem. We can do this because of the phenomenon of habit.

Whether we realize it or not, our habits play a significant part in our spiritual formation and the spiritual formation of our families. Our households are not simply products of what we teach and say. They are much more the products of what we practice and do. For example, most of us parents want to be patient, attentive, gentle, and loving toward our kids. But until our hopes make their way from our heads to our habits, nothing will change. The idea of the parents we want to be will remain stuck in our minds—and our kids will suffer as a result.

But it doesn't have to be that way. It is possible to practice habits of the household that lead our hearts, and our children's hearts, in new directions. I've seen this happen in my own parenting life. For instance, it used to be that when my kids spilled something, I immediately reprimanded them, which led to an impatient mood of constantly snapping at them. I had to cultivate a new habit of saying (often through gritted teeth), "That's okay. Why don't you help me clean it up?" This led to me *feeling* more patient because I *practiced* talking patiently.

Now, let me be careful and clear in saying this wasn't an immediate or easy process. Likewise, it won't necessarily be easy or immediate for you to implement these habits in your household. Nothing important ever is easy. But I will say that changing these habits is *possible.*

What's more, you are not alone in the journey. The Christian posture toward habits of the household is not about carrying your family on your back and hiking up the steep mountain of life. It is much more childlike than that. It is simply about taking hold of the outstretched hand of your heavenly Father and following him . . . one baby step at a time.

So don't worry. Rethinking the habits of your household isn't a heavy burden. What is heavy and burdensome is continuing to do *nothing*. Taking the hand of God and being willing to follow him wherever he leads—that's light. It's the posture of a child. Someone who is stronger than you and who loves you is in charge. And that's good news for parents and children.

—*Justin Whitmel Earley*

HOW TO USE THIS GUIDE

The big reality that sparked this study into life is that people become their habits. This is true for people generally, and it is true for you and me specifically. Scary, right? Well, here is something even more frightening: not only do you become your habits, but your children also become you. Your habits have a huge impact on your kids.

This is why we are going to spend the next several weeks exploring the *habits of the household*—those daily routines we do that have such a big impact on our families. We are going to see how intentionally harnessing the most routine moments in our lives can pay huge dividends not only in our own spiritual formation but in the lives of those we love most.

Now, before you begin, keep in mind that there are a few ways you can go through this material. You can experience this study with others in a group (such as a Bible study, Sunday school class, or any other small-group gathering), or you may choose to go through the content on your own. Either way, know that the videos for each session are available for you to view at any time via streaming by following the instructions provided with this study guide.

GROUP STUDY

Each of the sessions in this study are divided into two parts: (1) a group study section, and (2) a personal study section. The group study section provides a basic framework on how to open your time together, get the most out of the video content, and discuss the key ideas that were presented in the teaching. Each session includes the following:

- **Welcome:** A short opening note about the topic of the session for you to read on your own before you meet as a group.
- **Connect:** A few icebreaker questions to get you and your group members thinking about the topic and interacting with each other.
- **Watch:** An outline of the key points covered in each video teaching along with space for you to take notes as you watch each session.
- **Discuss:** Questions to help you and your group reflect on the teaching material presented and apply it to your lives.
- **Respond:** A short personal exercise to help reinforce the key ideas.
- **Pray:** A place to record requests that you will pray about during the week.

If you are doing this study in a group, make sure you have your own copy of the study guide so you can write down your thoughts, responses, and reflections—and so you have access to the videos via streaming. You will also want to have a copy of *Habits of the Household*, as reading it alongside the curriculum will provide you with deeper insights. (See the notes at the beginning of each group session and personal study section on which chapters of the book you should read before the next group session.)

Finally, keep these points in mind:

- **Facilitation:** If you are doing this study in a group, you will want to appoint someone to serve as a facilitator. This person will take the lead on starting the video and keeping track of time during discussions and activities. If you have been chosen for this role, there are some resources in the back of this guide that can help you lead your group through the study.

- **Faithfulness:** Your group is a place where tremendous growth can happen as you reflect on the Bible, ask questions, and learn what God is doing in other people's lives. For this reason, be fully committed and attend each session so you can build trust and rapport with the other members.

- **Friendship:** The goal of any small group is to serve as a place where people can share, learn about God, and build friendships. So seek to make your group a safe place by being honest about your thoughts and feelings, but also by listening carefully to everyone else in the group. Keep anything personal that your group members share in confidence so that you can create an authentic community where people can heal, be challenged, and grow spiritually.

If you are going through this study on your own, read the opening Welcome section and reflect on the questions in the Connect section. Watch the video and use the outline provided to take notes. Finally, personalize the questions and exercises in the Discuss and Respond sections. Close by recording any requests you want to pray about during the week.

PERSONAL STUDY

The personal study is for you to go work through on your own during the week. Each exercise is designed to help you explore the key ideas you uncovered during your group time and delve into passages of Scripture that will help you apply those principles to your life. Go at your own pace, doing a little each day—or tackle the material all at once. Remember to spend a few moments in silence to listen to whatever God might be saying to you.

Note that if you are doing this study as part of a group, and you are unable to finish (or even start) these personal studies for the week, you should still attend the group time. Be assured that you are still wanted and welcome even if you don't have your "homework" done. The group studies and personal studies are intended to help you hear what God wants you to hear and how to apply what he is saying to your life. So . . . as you go through this study, be listening for him to speak to you about the habits he wants you to have in your household.

WEEKEND RETREAT

If you are the group leader, you might want to consider planning a *Habits of the Household* weekend retreat for couples in your group or in your church. Refer to the Leader's Guide at the back of this study guide for options and tips on how to make this happen. The weekend retreat will require some planning, but you will find that the attendees will benefit greatly from it.

SCHEDULE
WEEK 1

BEFORE GROUP MEETING	Read chapters 1 and 10 in *Habits of the Household* Read the Welcome section (page 13)
GROUP MEETING	Discuss the Connect questions Watch the video teaching for session 1 Discuss the questions that follow as a group Do the closing exercise and pray (pages 13–21)
STUDY 1	Complete the personal study (pages 25–27)
STUDY 2	Complete the personal study (pages 28–30)
STUDY 3	Complete the personal study (pages 31–33)
CONNECT AND DISCUSS	Connect with someone in your group (page 34)
CATCH UP AND READ AHEAD **(BEFORE WEEK 2 GROUP MEETING)**	Read chapters 2 and 5 in *Habits of the Household* Complete any unfinished personal studies (page 35)

WAKING UP TO HABITS OF THE HOUSEHOLD

I lie down and sleep; I wake again, because the Lord sustains me. I will not fear though tens of thousands assail me on every side.

PSALM 3:5–6

The main measure of your devotion to
God is not your devotional life.
It is simply your life.

JOHN ORTBERG[1]

We are what we repeatedly do.
Excellence, then, is not
an act, but a habit.

WILL DURANT[2]

WELCOME [read on your own]

Did you know your brain is designed for habits? Without getting too technical, habits are formed in the deepest part of our brains, called the basal ganglia. This is the part of our brains that allow us to operate on autopilot—doing routine tasks like tying our shoes or washing the dishes without us even really thinking about what we are doing.

Habits are necessary for life as we know it. They free up our minds to focus on the more important stuff, like relationships and challenges at work, even as we perform routines such as driving a car, folding laundry, or walking without falling down. Habits are so powerful that we drift into them without conscious thought.

The problem is that not all habits are good. Some are even negative and harmful. This can include everything from biting our fingernails, to eating sweets, to lashing out in anger. We can carry out these harmful habits without even realizing we are doing so. And they are difficult to change, because we develop habits by practicing them over and over (often unconsciously), so we can't just *think* our way out of a habit. We can only remove bad habits—or replace them with good ones—by practicing routines that we want to implement again and again.

This is the goal of this study: to help you learn how to intentionally harness the power of habits in ways that produce good for you and for those you love. In this opening session, we are going to start by looking at two routines that are biologically essential and shape everything else that we experience in a given day. Those routines are around *waking* and *sleeping*.

CONNECT [10 minutes]

If you or any of your group members don't know each other, take a few minutes to introduce yourselves. Then discuss one or both of the following questions:

- Why did you decide to join this study? What do you hope to learn?

    —*or*—

- What is an example of a habit or routine that has impacted your life?

WATCH [20 minutes]

Now watch the video for this session, which you can access by playing the DVD or through streaming (see the instructions provided with this guide). Below is an outline of the key points covered during the teaching. Record any key concepts that stand out to you.

Outline

I. At times in our lives, we gain an epiphany of what it is like to live with *us*.

    A. Realizing what the "normal" is for ourselves and our family can be discouraging.

    B. But there are liturgies we can implement to change our normal.

    C. A new normal can be achieved through the power of a good parenting habit.

II. God will do some of his most extraordinary spiritual work in the ordinary hallways of family life.

    A. We live in a household filled with habits. The question is: *what habits do we want to have?*

    B. This question is critical because we become our habits—and then our children become us.

    C. When we are honest about our messy normal, it opens us up to receiving God's grace.

III. Habit #1: A kneeling prayer right beside our bed as soon as we wake up.

    A. It's easy to start the day thinking about everything we need to do—but it's not helpful.

    B. A morning prayer starts the day by refocusing on what God has already done.

    C. The point is to start the day with what God has done so we can follow his lead.

IV. Habit #2: Go to Scripture before phone (or any other distraction).

    A. This simply means to eliminate the phone from our morning routines.

    B. If we start the day with news and notifications, we will feel anxious about the world.

    C. It is so much better to start the day with wisdom from God's Word.

V. Habit #3: Morning prayer with our children.

    A. A morning prayer intentionally invites our children into discipleship.

    B. These prayers should be simple and practical rather than extravagant and fancy.

C. Little moments in the routine can bring enormous changes in the family's life.

Notes

Scripture Before Phone

Commit to implementing a set of practices in your home that make a habit of ignoring your phone in the morning and going to the Bible instead. Tips to start:

- Set your phone to Do Not Disturb so you don't see notifications upon waking. Also set an alarm or change the wallpaper on your phone to remind you.

- Make it a routine to go to the same couch or chair each morning. Place your Bible and a journal nearby so that they are readily accessible.

- Follow a reading plan or a devotional, ideally with your spouse or others.

- Be comfortable with brief readings and prayers as the norm, but let the habit grow to longer times as permitted on weekends or slower days.

- Lean toward a print Bible, but if you use a Scripture app, use voice activation to open it so you don't get distracted with other things on your phone.

- When just beginning, tell a friend or spouse that you are trying to develop this habit so they can help keep you accountable. Ideally, try thirty days together.

- Don't get mad when you mess up. Habits are norms, not rules.

 # Ideas for Morning Kneeling Prayers

Briefly, and beside the bed:

- Lord, thank you for the gift of another day. Help me walk with your love into whatever work you have called me to today. Amen.

- Lord, thank you for the gift of a day with the ones you have given me to love. Be among us as we work at play and work at love. Amen.

- Lord, please help. Remind me of your power in my weakness as I try to love others, despite my exhaustion. Amen.

DISCUSS [40 minutes]

Discuss what you just watched by answering the following questions.

1. An *epiphany* can be defined as "an intuitive grasp of reality through something (such as an event) usually simple and striking."[3] When have you experienced an epiphany in your life about something that was not working? What brought about that epiphany?

2. We all have an idea of what is considered "normal" in our households—those routines, actions, and attitudes that are typically experienced in our homes. What are some words that describe what "normal" looks like in your household right now?

3. The wonderful reality for each of us is that God will do some of his most profound and extraordinary spiritual work within the ordinary rhythms and routines of ordinary homes. When has that been true in your life—both as a child and now as an adult?

4. In the video, we explored three potential new habits for waking up: (1) a kneeling prayer by the bed, (2) always putting Scripture before phone, and (3) a morning prayer with our children. Which of those three strikes you as most potentially helpful in your household?

5. Bedtime is a moment for both parent and child to acknowledge that at the end of the day, God loves us. The following page contains several suggestions for simple bedtime liturgies and blessings. Which of these are most interesting or different to you? Right now, what are some of the bigger challenges or obstacles that make bedtime frustrating in your household?

A Tickle Blessing

Suddenly, and with lots of squirming:

Parent: Dear Lord, may this child find much joy and laughter, all of his/her days.
Child: Uncontrollable laughter, until they can barely breathe.
Parent: Amen.

A Bouncy Blessing

While bouncing around the child, and trying to get as much giggling and flopping as possible:

Parent: Lord, may this child bounce from blessing to blessing, all of his/her days.
Child: Bouncing and laughing
Parent: Amen.

A Blessing for the Body

As prayer progresses, move hands to touch each part of the body:

Jesus, **bless their feet,** may they bring good news.
Bless their legs, may they carry on in times of suffering.
Bless their backs, may they be strong enough to bear the burdens of others.
Bless their arms to hold the lonely, **and their hands** to do good work.
Bless their necks, may they turn their heads toward the poor.
Bless their ears to discern truth, **their eyes** to see beauty, and **their mouths**
    to speak encouragement.
Bless their minds, may they grow wise.
And finally, **bless their hearts,** may they grow to love you—and all that you
    have made—in the right order. Amen.

RESPOND [10 minutes]

For centuries, Jewish families have followed their own "habits of the household" by reciting the *Shema* out loud each day. This prayer, recorded in Deuteronomy 6:4–9, was originally offered by Moses after he restated the Ten Commandments to the Israelites while they gathered on the outskirts of the Promised Land. Jesus quoted a portion of this same passage when one of the scribes of his day asked him to identify the most important commandment in Scripture (see Mark 12:29–30). Here is the passage from the book of Deuteronomy:

> Hear, O Israel: The Lord our God, the Lord is one. Love the Lord your God with all your heart and with all your soul and with all your strength. These commandments that I give you today are to be on your hearts. Impress them on your children. Talk about them when you sit at home and when you walk along the road, when you lie down and when you get up. Tie them as symbols on your hands and bind them on your foreheads. Write them on the doorframes of your houses and on your gates.
>
> *Deuteronomy 6:4–9*

Where do you see connections between these verses and the themes described in the video?

What are some habits or routines that come to mind when you think about impressing God's Word on your heart as you sit at home, walk along the road, lie down, and get up?

PRAY [10 minutes]

Praying for one another is one of the most important things you can do as a community. So make this time more than just a "closing prayer" to end your group experience by vulnerably sharing your prayers and asking God to reveal life-changing opportunities that will help you instill new habits over the next few weeks. Use the space below to write down any prayer requests so you and your group members can pray about them in the week ahead.

NAME   **REQUEST**

PERSONAL STUDY

We all live in homes filled with habits. In fact, the question is not whether we have habits but what kinds of habits we have. This is why it is important for us to take a look at the habits we have established in our homes to see if they are leading us and our families toward spiritual maturity or away from it. This is the goal of these personal studies—to provide you with a place to make this assessment. As you work through the exercises, be sure to write down your responses to the questions, as you will be given a few minutes to share your insights at the start of the next session if you are doing this study with others. If you are reading *Habits of the Household* alongside this study, first review the Introduction and chapters 1 and 10 of the book.

THE FOUNDATION

As mentioned in the group time, we are going to be spending a lot of time and attention in this study focusing on habits, routines, liturgies, and other "regular" elements in our lives and in our homes. These explorations will be highly practical. Yet it is also important to start this study by exploring the root and foundation that undergirds all of those "regular" activities.

This root and foundation is *love*. First, it is the love that we experience from our heavenly Father. Remember, before we become parents, we are first children—specifically, children of God. His love for us undergirds everything we do within our households.

Second, it is the love between us as people, including love for our spouses and love for our kids. And, yes, given the realities of our culture, that also includes the love and grace we show one another as ex-spouses, step-parents, step-children, in-laws, and the like. Everything that touches our homes must be rooted in love.

So, as we prepare to explore all the different habits that can have a positive impact on our households, let's remember these important words from the apostle Peter: "Above all, love each other deeply, because love covers over a multitude of sins. Offer hospitality to one another without grumbling. Each of you should use whatever gift you have received to serve others, as faithful stewards of God's grace in its various forms" (1 Peter 4:8–10).

HABITS OF THE HOUSEHOLD

1. As an academic concept, *love* can be hard to define or pin down. But most of us have an innate ability to recognize the presence of love when we encounter it—or the absence of love when we don't. Growing up in your household as a child, what routines or practices were especially meaningful to you? What made you feel loved?

2. Now as an adult, what are some of the primary ways you experience love within your household? What are some of the primary ways you express love to those closest to you?

Realizing that the normal moments of life are also the most spiritual moments of life helps give a validity and dignity to the otherwise mundane and repetitive nature of housework and parenting. I know we parents constantly wonder whether all of this matters, and I will try to assure you over and over: yes, it does! Your work in the household and parenting matters tremendously. It will echo into eternity.

But on the other hand, this is challenging because it reminds us of why parenting is so very, very hard. Parenting, seen properly, is an unceasing spiritual battle. A battle that God is using to refine us, and a battle that God will win for us, but if it feels like a fight to you, that's because it is.[4]

3. In what ways does participation in your household feel like a "battle" or a "fight" right now? What do you think might be the root causes of those struggles?

You will, inevitably, at times while going through this study be tempted to wonder, "Isn't this legalistic? Isn't it the power of God that changes us, not the power of our habits?" I will try to remind you that no, it is not legalistic. And yes, it is the power of God that changes us, habits included. . . .

Caring about how habits are shaping your family is not legalistic. What would be legalistic is saying that God loves you more because of your habits. Or that you can earn your salvation by picking the right habits. You can't. And thank God, you don't need to!

The good news of Christianity is that Jesus' death on the cross has paid for all of our failures (including our bad parenting habits), and his resurrection from the grave is the promise of a new life (including new parenting habits). It is that work of God that saves us, by grace and through faith—not our works (of habits or otherwise). That God died for us while we were still sinners is a demonstration of his great love, and that love is why we care about habits.[5]

4. Building helpful habits and routines is a critical element within a healthy household, but those habits are not the end goal. The end goal is joining in God's work and God's love. Where do you currently see God at work within your home?

5. What are your goals for participating in this study? What would you like to see changed or developed within your household as a result of working through these pages?

HABITS AROUND WAKING

Waking up each day is one of those routines we often take for granted. Sometimes we open our eyes refreshed and ready for whatever may come our way. Other times we are groggy or tired or even resentful at the necessity of rolling out of the covers. It is easy to believe that whatever side of the spectrum on which we fall—whether or not we "wake up on the wrong side of the bed"—isn't really important and depends on factors beyond our control.

But the truth is that the way we wake up does matter. It matters to us as individuals in terms of how we approach everything that will happen throughout the rest of the day. And it matters to the other members of our household who look to us for guidance and support.

It is also true that we have a lot of control over the way we wake up. Or, at least, we have a lot of control over what we experience the first moments after we wake up. All too often we jump immediately into a human-centered version of reality by checking email, watching the news, clicking on what others are doing through social media, or jumping immediately into the never-ending list of chores that need to be completed each day. Making that decision has tremendous impact on our thoughts and actions throughout the rest of the day.

A more helpful approach is to immediately jump into the true version of reality that is centered on God. We can do this through many means, including prayer, worship, meditation, and exposure to his Word. As the apostle Paul wrote to one group of believers, "Wake up, sleeper, rise from the dead, and Christ will shine on you" (Ephesians 5:14).

1. What are some words that describe your typical "wake up" routine over the past several months? What emotions do you typically experience the first minutes of a typical day?

2. The way we start the day as individuals is important, but each of our individual choices also contributes to the overall environment of our household. So, what are some words that describe the typical "wake up" experience in your household over the past several months? What is the overall attitude or atmosphere in your home on a typical morning?

At best, the morning rituals of a household support the reality that God loves us and that his love is the defining fact of the universe. Here our habits of waking serve as gospel liturgies that push us into the arms of a father who loves us, and then send us out into the world to love others. But at worst, our habits of waking indulge alternative realities where the universe depends on us and what we do today. This is the gospel of humankind, where our rituals tell us that we have to keep up to survive and turn the household into a school of rush, fear, and frustration.

So we must wake up to how we wake up. We must see that the first role of a parent is not to get everyone up on time but to root our household habits of waking in the truth of the gospel. For in the story of God, our call is not simply to wake up our bodies each day but to awaken our hearts to God's love.[6]

3. Waking up well is both a challenge and an opportunity. Where do you see opportunities to experience God's love each morning? What about the others in your household—where do you see opportunities to help them experience God's love at the start of each day?

Let the morning bring me word of your unfailing love, for I have put my trust in you. Show me the way I should go, for to you I entrust my life.

Psalm 143:8

"So do not worry, saying, 'What shall we eat?' or 'What shall we drink?' or 'What shall we wear?' For the pagans run after all these things, and your heavenly Father knows that you need them. But seek first his kingdom and his righteousness, and all these things will be given to you as well."

Matthew 6:31–33

Start children off on the way they should go, and even when they are old they will not turn from it.

Proverbs 22:6

4. In the group time this week, we looked at three morning routines: (1) a kneeling prayer upon waking, (2) Scripture before phone, and (3) a morning prayer with our children. What do these passages say about the importance of these morning routines?

5. You know your household better than anyone else, which means you have an expert understanding of what your household needs. What are some additional morning routines that you could implement to bring about a "new normal" in your home?

HABITS AROUND BEDTIME

As we have seen, each morning presents a new opportunity for us to recognize the goodness of God's love and the reality of his presence in our lives. The presence of the Lord is even pictured every day by the natural world. Dawn is a wonderful illustration of God's light breaking through the darkness and penetrating throughout every area of our lives.

In a similar way, nighttime offers wonderful opportunities for us and our families to use the natural rhythms of the day as a means of reinforcing core truths. Even as the sun goes down and our homes are once again plunged into darkness, we can affirm the reality that God is with us even in the darkest and the bleakest times in our lives. God is present with each of us individually, and God is present within our households.

When unmanaged, bedtime rituals can become times of chaos. Kids who don't want to brush their teeth or clean their rooms or hop into bed will do anything to disrupt those expected routines. Parents who are exhausted from the work of the day often lose patience in those moments. Nighttime can be a bit of a mess. But when managed well, bedtime can become a reassuring routine—one filled with comfort and acceptance for the blessing of rest.

1. What are some words that describe a typical bedtime in your household—specifically the final thirty minutes before the children are supposed to be in bed? What emotions are most likely to be experienced by you and your family in those minutes?

2. Take a moment to think about the perfect bedtime experience for yourself and your family—an ideal end to the day. Use the space below to sketch out that ideal bedtime, either visually or with words. What would your routines look like? What would be said? What other senses would be involved (touch, smell, taste)? What emotions?

A good parent can settle the soul—and that's exactly what our heavenly father can do for us. Send us to bed with a settled soul. I find that I need this reminder the most at the end of the day, when all of us are exhausted and running on reserves. This is when I need gospel liturgies to guide me into rest, body and soul.

But just like all these habits of the household, bedtime liturgies aren't solutions to make bedtime easy or prevent us from being bad parents, they are rhythms that remind us we can rest in God's goodness anyway. And we need those. Because otherwise we get stuck in our anger, our self-loathing, and our failures. That's why I try to repeat this statement as often as possible: Our habits won't change God's love for us, but God's love for us can and should change our habits.[7]

3. *A good parent can settle the soul.* Think back to a recent evening where this did not happen—a bedtime that reflected more chaos than comfort. With the benefit of hindsight, what steps could you have taken that might have improved that evening?

For those who are led by the Spirit of God are the children of God. The Spirit you received does not make you slaves, so that you live in fear again; rather, the Spirit you received brought about your adoption to sonship. And by him we cry, "Abba, Father." The Spirit himself testifies with our spirit that we are God's children. Now if we are children, then we are heirs—heirs of God and co-heirs with Christ, if indeed we share in his sufferings in order that we may also share in his glory.

Romans 8:14–17

4. Our best parenting comes when we think less about being parents of children and more about being children of God. What are some examples of grace that God has demonstrated to you? What does it mean that God is our heavenly "Father"?

5. Liturgies and blessings are good options for helping your household wind down and end each day well, but not the only options. Take a moment to think specifically about your needs and the needs of your children. What are some other routines you could implement in your household that could be helpful for ending the day well?

CONNECT AND DISCUSS

Take some time today to connect with a fellow group member and discuss some of the key insights from this first session. Use any of the following prompts to help guide your discussion.

What stood out to you the most from the content in this session? Why?

A central principle of this study is that God will do his most transformational work within the boundaries of ordinary homes. How have you seen that principle at work this week?

Take a moment to talk through some of the "waking" habits suggested in this week's teaching. Which ones are you most excited to try in your household? Why?

Now think about some of the bedtime blessings and liturgies mentioned. Which of those particularly caught your attention? Why?

What do you feel most excited to explore or learn in the sessions ahead?

CATCH UP AND READ AHEAD

Use this time to go back and complete any of the study and reflection questions from previous days that you weren't able to finish. Make a note below of any revelations you've had and reflect on any growth or personal insights you've gained.

Make sure to read chapters 2 and 5 in *Habits of the Household* before the next group gathering. Use the space below to make note of anything in those chapters that stands out to you or encourages you.

SCHEDULE
WEEK 2

BEFORE GROUP MEETING	Read chapters 2 and 5 in *Habits of the Household* Read the Welcome section (page 39)
GROUP MEETING	Discuss the Connect questions Watch the video teaching for session 2 Discuss the questions that follow as a group Do the closing exercise and pray (pages 39–47)
STUDY 1	Complete the daily study (pages 51–53)
STUDY 2	Complete the daily study (pages 54–56)
STUDY 3	Complete the daily study (pages 57–59)
CONNECT AND DISCUSS	Connect with someone in your group (page 60)
CATCH UP AND READ AHEAD (BEFORE WEEK 3 GROUP MEETING)	Read chapters 4 and 8 in *Habits of the Household* Complete any unfinished personal studies (page 61)

HABITS FOR MEALTIMES AND FAMILY DEVOTIONS

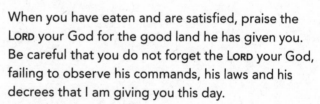

When you have eaten and are satisfied, praise the LORD your God for the good land he has given you. Be careful that you do not forget the LORD your God, failing to observe his commands, his laws and his decrees that I am giving you this day.

DEUTERONOMY 8:10–11

As long as we are thinking only of natural values the sun looks down on nothing half so good as a household laughing together over a meal.

C. S. LEWIS[8]

Nothing helps scenery like bacon and eggs.

MARK TWAIN[9]

WELCOME [read on your own]

One of the goals for this session is to explore different ways to harness those moments when your family gathers together as a household—specifically at mealtimes and for communal devotionals. But even the idea of gathering together as a household can seem like a challenge in today's culture. Why? Because families are more siloed and separated now than ever before.

According to recent studies, about seventy percent of meals are consumed outside of the home for families in the United States. About twenty percent of those meals are eaten inside a car. Most disturbing of all, about half of American families "rarely" have dinner together.[10] So, the first step in establishing mealtime as a healthy habit in our households is to make it a priority to establish mealtime as a family event. We need to eat together. Regularly. We need to make the dinner table a central spot for the household. When that becomes a priority, we will open the door to a whole range of meaningful moments and significant surprises.

Another meaningful moment that dovetails neatly with mealtimes is family devotions. This tends to be a scary thought for many parents today (and for many children as well). But the same God who established the *Shema* also said, "Let the little children come to me, and do not hinder them, for the kingdom of God belongs to such as these" (Luke 18:16).

Therefore, we have both a meaningful responsibility and a wonderful opportunity to create rhythms of spiritual education and formation within our households—rhythms that can pay dividends not only for years or decades, but also for eternity.

CONNECT [10 minutes]

Take a few minutes to catch up with your fellow group members. Then choose one or both of the following questions to discuss as a group:

- What is something that spoke to your heart in last week's personal study that you would like to share with the group?

  —*or*—

- On a scale of 1 (low) to 10 (high), how comfortable would you feel leading daily devotions for your family for a week? Why?

WATCH [20 minutes]

Now watch the video for this session. Below is an outline of the key points covered during the teaching. Record any key concepts that stand out to you.

Outline

I. We can transform the table into the center of gravity for family life.
   A. It is easy to make our schedules the center of everything.
   B. Jesus said the center of life is relationships: loving God and loving others.
   C. Two rhythms are key to relationships: family meals and family devotions.

II. What is spiritual about mealtimes?
   A. The places we feel are mundane are often where the majority of our formation takes place.
   B. We need to learn to look at life through a liturgical lens.
   C. Everyday meals are filled with liturgies and opportunities for significance.
   D. At the table, we're reminded that ordinary life with each other is spiritual life with God.

III. There are a few habits you can employ to help you find each other at the dinner table.
   A. Habit #1: Consider engaging in some conversational rhythms.
   B. Habit #2: Consider having the family involved in preparing meals and clean up.
   C. Habit #3: Consider making hospitality a part of your weekly rhythm.

IV. The table also presents a great opportunity for loving God through family devotions.
   A. Even the term "family devotions" can feel scary and overwhelming to some.
   B. Remember that family devotions don't need to be perfect—they just need to happen.
   C. Family devotions work best when we are okay with things getting a bit messy.

V. There are a few habits you can employ to help you start regular family devotions.
   A. Habit #1: Try starting with a snack or dessert right at the table.
   B. Habit #2: Use simple Scriptures—you don't need deep theological lessons.
   C. Habit #3: Think about rhythms of short prayers—prayer requests and family participation.

Notes

_____

_____

_____

_____

_____

_____

_____

_____

_____

_____

_____

_____

_____

_____

_____

_____

_____

_____

_____

_____

_____

_____

_____

_____

_____

_____

_____

_____

_____

_____

_____

_____

Conversational Rhythms for the Table

Try any of the below as norms for teaching the practice of conversation.

- Devices, for parents or kids, are not allowed at dinner, not even in pockets or on the table. They are silenced and somewhere else.

- Pass the pepper, or other object, and have everyone answer the same question. After going once around the table, ask a new question.

- For bigger families with older children, try the "One Conversation Rule." You can talk about anything, but everyone has to be talking about the same thing.

- Have everyone answer the same set of questions—for example, sharing one good thing and one bad thing. Add one funny thing for humor. If it's breakfast, have everyone share one thing they are excited about for the day.

- As parents, try telling simple stories about your day. The art of learning to take life and put it into stories is something children can learn at the table.

- Ask specific questions. Instead of general questions like "How was school?" "What is one thing you did well today?" or "What made you mad today?"

DISCUSS [40 minutes]

Discuss what you just watched by answering the following questions.

1. How would you describe what mealtimes are currently like at your household?

2. One of the themes discussed in this week's teaching is that the table can become the "center of gravity" for life within a household. Why do you think this is the case? What would it look like to make the table the center of gravity in your own home?

3. What does it mean to look at family mealtimes through a "liturgical lens"? Why is it important to look underneath the chaos that might be happening at these mealtimes?

4. Think about the three habits that were discussed for mealtimes: (1) establishing conversational rhythms, (2) shared meal prep and clean up, and (3) extending hospitality to those outside the household. Which of those habits might fit well in your household? Which ones do you think would be more difficult for you to do on a regular basis? Why?

5. Family devotions can often be uncomfortable because parents feel unprepared for the task and children expect to be bored. In your experience, what are some helpful tips or tricks that you have found to turn family devotionals into a win for both parties?

Simple Scriptures and Short Prayers

Things to try for telling simple truths:

- Try reading or memorizing some lines of a catechism together. (For younger children, try the New City Catechism; for older children, try the Westminster Shorter Catechism.)[11] Start with one question-and-response a week.

- Go through the Lord's Prayer or the Apostles' Creed and explain the concepts. Again, one line a week is plenty of fodder.

- If you do family mottos, try basing one around a short passage of Scripture (e.g., "We Try to Be Strong and Courageous" or "We Try to Be Joyful Always").

- Memorize Scripture through music (e.g., Slugs & Bugs combines Scripture with some really great music that you will enjoy along with your kids).

Things to try for praying short prayers:

- Pray together when you find yourselves in need.

- Invite family members to pray before a meal.

- Pray for them, out loud, when they share something they feel or need.

- Pray together before school or bedtime.

- Pray together after a fight in the family happens.

RESPOND [10 minutes]

On the night before Jesus was betrayed and arrested, he made it a point to gather with his disciples for a last meal. The meal they shared, the Passover, required a number of provisions for both preparation and celebration, including avoiding yeast and cooking all the meat over an open fire. People even had to dress as if they were ready for a journey, with their cloaks tucked into their belts and their sandals on their feet. The goal was to commemorate what the Jewish nation experienced during the exodus from Egypt. Even so, what Jesus initiated during the Last Supper still offers some important principles or values that can be reflected in our family meals.

> When the hour came, Jesus and his apostles reclined at the table. And he said to them, "I have eagerly desired to eat this Passover with you before I suffer. For I tell you, I will not eat it again until it finds fulfillment in the kingdom of God."
>
> After taking the cup, he gave thanks and said, "Take this and divide it among you. For I tell you I will not drink again from the fruit of the vine until the kingdom of God comes."
>
> And he took bread, gave thanks and broke it, and gave it to them, saying, "This is my body given for you; do this in remembrance of me."
>
> In the same way, after the supper he took the cup, saying, "This cup is the new covenant in my blood, which is poured out for you. But the hand of him who is going to betray me is with mine on the table. The Son of Man will go as it has been decreed. But woe to that man who betrays him!" They began to question among themselves which of them it might be who would do this.
>
> A dispute also arose among them as to which of them was considered to be greatest. Jesus said to them, "The kings of the Gentiles lord it over them; and those who exercise authority over them call themselves Benefactors. But you are not to be like that. Instead, the greatest among you should be like the youngest, and the one who rules like the one who serves. For who is greater, the one who is at the table or the one who serves? Is it not the one who is at the table? But I am among you as one who serves. You are those who have stood by me in my trials. And I confer on you a kingdom, just as my Father conferred one on me, so that you may eat and drink at my table in my kingdom and sit on thrones, judging the twelve tribes of Israel."
>
> *Luke 22:14–30*

Where do you see Jesus establishing rituals or liturgies within this meal?

Where do you see the kind of messiness that we often experience at family mealtimes?

PRAY [10 minutes]

Conclude this session by thanking God for all the gifts that are wrapped into family meals and devotionals. Thank him for his provision (including your food), for the joy of time spent together, and for the opportunity to know him and know his Word even as you are known by those closest to you. Afterward, use the space below to write down any requests mentioned so that you and your group members can continue to pray about them in the week ahead.

NAME   **REQUEST**

_____   _____
_____   _____
_____   _____
_____   _____
_____   _____
_____   _____
_____   _____
_____   _____
_____   _____
_____   _____
_____   _____
_____   _____
_____   _____

PERSONAL STUDY

In this session, you examined another set of critical household rhythms that can produce great benefits for both parents and children alike: *mealtimes* and *devotions* (specifically, family devotions). You examined those routines on a general level during the group study time, but now you are going to shift the focus more specifically to your own household. As you work through the exercises in this personal study section, be sure to write down your responses to the questions, as you will be given a few minutes to share your insights at the start of the next session if you are doing this study with others. If you are reading *Habits of the Household* alongside this study, first review chapters 2 and 5 before completing the pages that follow.

MEALS IN SCRIPTURE

Have you ever thought about how often food is mentioned in the Bible? Not just uses of food as metaphors or word pictures—such as Jesus being the "bread of life"—but biblical references to the basic, biological phenomenon we call eating. Here are just a few examples:

> The LORD God commanded the man, "You are free to eat from any tree in the garden; but you must not eat from the tree of the knowledge of good and evil, for when you eat from it you will certainly die" (Genesis 2:16–17).

> The LORD said to Moses and Aaron, "Say to the Israelites: 'Of all the animals that live on land, these are the ones you may eat'" (Leviticus 11:1–2).

> "I am the seer," Samuel replied. "Go up ahead of me to the high place, for today you are to eat with me, and in the morning I will send you on your way and will tell you all that is in your heart" (1 Samuel 9:19).

> "Please test your servants for ten days: Give us nothing but vegetables to eat and water to drink. Then compare our appearance with that of the young men who eat the royal food, and treat your servants in accordance with what you see" (Daniel 1:12–13).

> While Jesus was having dinner at Matthew's house, many tax collectors and sinners came and ate with him and his disciples. When the Pharisees saw this, they asked his disciples, "Why does your teacher eat with tax collectors and sinners?" (Matthew 9:10–11).

These are just the tip of the iceberg. The Bible is filled with many more references to people eating—including the famous last meal that Jesus ate with his disciples before his betrayal, arrest, and crucifixion, which we celebrate today as the "Lord's Supper." All of these references to food in Scripture reveal the importance of this rhythm in our lives.

1. It's easy to understand eating as being important. After all, we can't survive long without food. It's more difficult to view eating as being *spiritually* important or significant. How do the verses listed above reveal the connection between eating and our spiritual lives?

2. The broader focus of this study is on the habits we incorporate as a household. But those habits begin with each of us as individuals. Where do you see opportunities to harness the rhythm of eating in a way that is helpful for spiritual growth? For worship?

[We] began with a claim that the most significant thing about any household is what is considered normal. Why is this so important? Because the normal is what shapes us the most, though we notice it the least. It is precisely the unremarkable nature of the normal that gives it such remarkable power. All of our unspoken values get hidden under the invisibility cloak of the ordinary. We think of our day-to-day routines as neutral simply because we see them so often. But putting on the liturgical lens allows us to lift that cloak and see what is happening when we don't think anything is happening. The liturgical lens allows us to see all of our normal moments for what they really are: moments of worship to someone or something. This pushes us to ask, "What exactly are we worshiping when we suppose we're not worshiping anything at all?"[12]

3. As you have worked through this study in recent weeks, how has your view of "regular" routines changed in your personal life? In your home life?

4. Communion is the primary example of establishing a connection between eating and spiritual formation. Read Paul's instructions for communion in 1 Corinthians 11:17–34. What specific principles did Paul establish for believers in Christ in those verses?

"When you fast, do not look somber as the hypocrites do, for they disfigure their faces to show others they are fasting. Truly I tell you, they have received their reward in full. But when you fast, put oil on your head and wash your face, so that it will not be obvious to others that you are fasting, but only to your Father, who is unseen; and your Father, who sees what is done in secret, will reward you."

Matthew 6:16–18

5. Fasting is another example of the connection between our physical and spiritual lives. What stands out to you about Jesus' instructions for that discipline? What opportunities do you have to incorporate fasting (from food and other things) into the rhythms of your life?

HABITS FOR MEALTIMES

For some time now, researchers have written about the benefits of "keystone habits." These are habits or routines that may seem small in and of themselves but that support a much wider variety of additional good habits. You might think of a keystone habit as the trunk of a tree—it's a healthy habit that branches out into many other healthy habits. Family mealtimes are such a keystone habit for healthy households (and for healthy individuals). When parents invest time and attention into establishing the regular routine of eating together as a family, they reap benefits for themselves and their children that go way beyond those mealtimes.

Yes, it's true that our schedules make breakfasts feel harried and harassed. And, yes, it's also true that many people are physically absent from the household at lunch because they are at school, at the office, running errands, and the like. So the keystone habit for your household may be as simple as declaring something similar to this principle: *We will sit down at our table and eat dinner together every night of the week with very few exceptions.*

Now, this doesn't mean just grabbing fast food and eating it in the car together as a family. This doesn't mean eating dinner on the couch with the television on. Nor is this a rotating system where some people eat after school and others grab some leftovers when practice is over. No, this *keystone habit* of family mealtime means everyone sitting down and focusing on the blessing of togetherness—of food and conversation and interaction and more. This one simple act can open the door to a world of blessing in your household.

1. In our modern culture, there are many obstacles that threaten or hinder our ability to experience a regular rhythm of family mealtimes. Which obstacles cause the most disruption to that keystone habit in your household?

2. What would you like family mealtimes to look like in your home? What specific routines would you like to incorporate? What kinds of foods? What types of conversations would you like to take place? Make a list below, and be specific.

Understanding that family habits are family liturgies clarifies where the work of worship and spiritual formation are actually happening—in the normal. For the most part, the place for this work is not in the moments we set aside as "spiritual." It is rather in the messy day-to-day patterns that the real work of spiritually formative parenting is done.

To me, this is freeing. I used to think I needed to get the day-to-day stuff done and out of the way to get to the real spiritual work of parenting—some special conversation where the magic would really happen. But now I see that the magic of God's grace abounds in the places I need it most: in the normal routines.

But this is also challenging because it suggests that we need to be comfortable with the mess if we're going to be serious about spiritual formation.[13]

3. Read 1 Corinthians 1:26–31. What does Paul say in this passage about how God uses the "foolish things of the world to shame the wise"? What does this say about the things that God will use in your life to reveal himself to you?

The biblical idea of the household enlarges family both in dimension and direction. In terms of dimension, the biblical concept of the household is simply larger. It included extended family, as well as people who were economically connected to your family—workers or neighbors on the same land, and so on.[14] But in terms of direction, the biblical concept of the household also pushes back on the idea of "family first."[15] We don't care for our household because our responsibility is to our bloodline and no one else—that is a cloaked form of tribalism. Rather, we care for the family because it is through the household that God's blessing to us is extended to others.

The biblical direction of blessing is always outward, not inward. We are blessed in order to bless others.[16] This ethic will run throughout all the habits of the household we discuss in this book, but there is no better place to begin than at the table, for the table is a place where we turn strangers into friends.[17]

4. How would you identify the boundaries of your "household"? Who is currently included in your household? Who else do you know who could be brought into it?

5. Eating a meal together as a family is a "normal" moment that has incredible potential for spiritual formation for you, your spouse, and your children. When has your family recently experienced a moment of grace or blessing at the table together?

FAMILY DEVOTIONS

There's an interesting moment recorded in the Gospels that illustrates the relationship between children and Jesus. In the book of Luke, that moment is recorded after a couple brief-but-interesting parables. First, Jesus talked about a widow who bothered a judge so persistently that he finally gave her justice. Second, Jesus talked about two people praying in the temple: a Pharisee who focused on his own self-righteousness and a tax collector who repented of his sin.

Both of those parables show the value of being comfortable with messiness in our spiritual lives—especially messy people. And both of those stories lead into this interesting encounter: "People were also bringing babies to Jesus for him to place his hands on them. When the disciples saw this, they rebuked them. But Jesus called the children to him and said, 'Let the little children come to me, and do not hinder them, for the kingdom of God belongs to such as these. Truly I tell you, anyone who will not receive the kingdom of God like a little child will never enter it'" (Luke 18:15–17).

As mentioned earlier, many parents feel hesitant at the idea of trying to lead family devotionals. Even afraid. The main source of that hesitancy is the fear that we won't do it "right" or that it won't be "perfect." We worry about our inability to accurately explain all the ins and outs of Scripture. We worry about our kids' inability to sit still long enough for something meaningful to take place. But let's stop worrying about those issues. Instead, like the parents mentioned in the Gospels, let's just find a way to bring our children closer to Jesus.

1. The basic goal of a family devotional points to something parents do all the time: teaching. What are some areas where you have been successful as a teacher or guide for your children?

2. Take a moment to write down your main goals for a family devotional experience. How often would you like to gather everyone for a devotional each week? What do you hope to experience? What would you like to teach or explore together?

The most radical truths are really simple ones. God is real. He loves you. Good and evil exist. Good will win. You are made in the image of God. You are also fallen. Jesus died for you. He also rose for you. God's world is beautiful. We are tasked with caring for it. Men and women exist. Families happen when they unite. Families are like building blocks of a healthy world; we should try to keep them together, and not topple them over. Prayer is real; it changes you as much as it changes the world. Life is hard, but God is with you. Suffering will happen, but it will sanctify you. Love is not a feeling, it is a sacrifice, usually in small things. God loves you, period. Your good deeds won't change that; your bad deeds won't change that. I will never leave you. Neither will Mom.

These are the life-altering paradigms that come in just a couple of words, once every Wednesday night. The rest of the week is about living them out, yes, but how powerful is it to find a moment in the week to just say one of them out loud?

3. Leading a family devotional does not require you to be a theological expert or even have answers to potential questions that may be asked. It's more about communicating simple truths. What are the simple truths your household needs to hear or engage with most?

4. During the group time, you looked at a variety of helpful suggestions for the habit of family devotions—including simple truths, short prayers, and catechisms. Which of those practical options seem helpful for your household right now? Why those in particular?

> "Fix these words of mine in your hearts and minds; tie them as symbols on your hands and bind them on your foreheads. Teach them to your children, talking about them when you sit at home and when you walk along the road, when you lie down and when you get up. Write them on the doorframes of your houses and on your gates, so that your days and the days of your children may be many in the land the LORD swore to give your ancestors, as many as the days that the heavens are above the earth."
>
> *Deuteronomy 11:18–21*

5. As parents, we have the privilege of teaching our children about God and his ways—and there's no time like the present to start teaching those lessons to our kids. With this in mind, use the space below to make a quick outline of a family devotional that you will lead this week. Be sure to include what content you will use (Scripture, devotional books, and the like), what questions you will ask, and what elements you plan to add (like snacks).

CONNECT AND DISCUSS

Take some time today to connect with a fellow group member and discuss some of the key insights from this session. Use any of the following prompts to help guide your discussion.

What ideas or concepts felt confusing from the study material within this session? What questions would you like to have answered?

Talk with each other about your current experiences with family mealtimes. What is going well? Where would you like to see growth or improvement?

This session focused on the messiness of life within our households. When have you seen messes or problems create an opportunity for growth within your home?

What are some specific goals you would like to achieve within your household when it comes to making the table your "center of gravity"? What goals for mealtimes? For devotionals?

What outside resources do you have experience with when it comes to something like family devotions? Which would you recommend to others?

CATCH UP AND READ AHEAD

Use this time to go back and complete any of the study and reflection questions from previous days that you weren't able to finish. Make a note below of any revelations you've had and reflect on any growth or personal insights you've gained.

Make sure you read chapters 4 and 8 in *Habits of the Household* before the next group gathering. Use the space below to make note of anything in those chapters that stands out to you or encourages you.

SCHEDULE
WEEK 3

BEFORE GROUP MEETING	Read chapters 4 and 8 in *Habits of the Household* Read the Welcome section (page 65)
GROUP MEETING	Discuss the Connect questions Watch the video teaching for session 3 Discuss the questions that follow as a group Do the closing exercise and pray (pages 65–73)
STUDY 1	Complete the daily study (pages 77–79)
STUDY 2	Complete the daily study (pages 80–83)
STUDY 3	Complete the daily study (pages 84–87)
CONNECT AND DISCUSS	Connect with someone in your group (page 88)
CATCH UP AND READ AHEAD **(BEFORE WEEK 4 GROUP MEETING)**	Read chapters 3 and 9 in *Habits of the Household* Complete any unfinished personal studies (page 89)

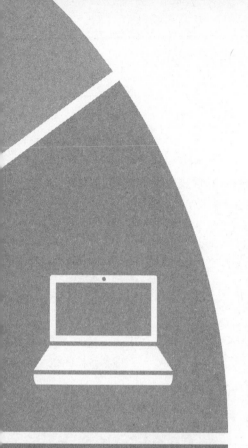

HABITS FOR SCREENTIME AND FORMATION

Finally, brothers and sisters, whatever is true, whatever is noble, whatever is right, whatever is pure, whatever is lovely, whatever is admirable—if anything is excellent or praiseworthy—think about such things.

PHILIPPIANS 4:8

Life in the digital age is an open invitation for clear, biblical thinking about the impact of our phones on ourselves, on our creation, on our neighbors, and on our relationships to God.

TONY REINKE[18]

Everyone is in a process of spiritual formation. We are being shaped into either the wholeness of the image of Christ or a horribly destructive caricature of that image.

ROBERT MULHOLLAND, JR.[19]

WELCOME [read on your own]

In November 2021, a landmark article written by researcher Jonathan Haidt exposed what he called "The Dangerous Experiment on Teen Girls." Haidt was specifically writing about the effects of social media on girls and young women. As he wrote, "Much more than for boys, adolescence typically heightens girls' self-consciousness about their changing body and amplifies insecurities about where they fit in their social network. . . . Social media takes the worst parts of middle school and glossy women's magazines and intensifies them."[20]

Haidt revealed that rates of depression and anxiety among teenagers have risen sharply in the past decade, with that rise beginning around the year 2011. Those rates mirrored similar rises in suicide and self-harm, and they seemed to be especially prominent among girls. "The timing points to social media," Haidt concluded.[21] Incredibly, Haidt also pointed to research that showed young girls were aware of the harm that social media platforms were causing in their lives—that they felt worse about themselves the more they used those platforms.

Haidt's research is just the tip of the iceberg when it comes to understanding how screens influence our lives. This is because that influence is not limited to just social media. What we experience through technology plays a huge role in shaping the way we think, what we value, how we behave, and who we are. Therefore, making responsible decisions around screentime is a critical part of creating healthy rhythms and habits within our households.

CONNECT [10 minutes]

Get the session started by choosing one or both of the following questions to discuss together as a group:

- What is something that spoke to your heart in last week's personal study that you would like to share with the group?

—or—

- Growing up, who were some of the biggest influences in your life? Who helped you to become the person you are today?

WATCH [20 minutes]

Now watch the video for this session. Below is an outline of the key points covered during the teaching. Record any key concepts that stand out to you.

Outline

I. Paying attention to the screen is not how we pay attention to life.
  A. It's easy to fall into the trap of allowing screens to be a convenient babysitter.
  B. It is critical to rethink our daily habits—primarily technology and screen time habits.
  C. Remember this exploration of screens and formation is about grace not judgment.

II. The fight over screentime is a fight over who is actually forming our lives.
  A. If we don't form our screentime rhythms, our screentime rhythms will form us.
  B. Screens are ready and willing to teach our families about all kinds of important subjects.
  C. The stakes of formation is high—which is why we need to be aware of screentime habits.

III. We need to implement a new paradigm for thinking about screentime decisions.
  A. Curation means setting limits and then choosing carefully within those limits.
  B. Limits are actually what allows us to choose on purpose when it comes to screentime.

IV. Three guiding principles for curation:
  A. Principle 1: Rhythms over rules.
    1. Establish rhythms of *on* time.
    2. Establish rhythms of *off* time.
    3. Remember that grace is better than legalism.
  B. Principle 2: Medium over message.
    1. Practice rhythms of discussion.
    2. Practice rhythms of patience.
    3. Choose the message well.
  C. Principle 3: Communal over individual.
    1. Share screentime together as a family.
    2. Practice rhythms of transparency.

V. When it comes to screentime, a parent's sacrifice is more important than a child's pain.
  A. The process of establishing limits on screentime is not easy for anyone.
  B. The good news of the gospel is that Jesus took the pain so we could have good lives.
  C. Likewise, parents need to do the hard things so their children can thrive.

Notes

Things to Consider in Setting Rhythms of On and Off Times for Screens

Note: Your rhythms may be different than other people's and may vary in seasons.

- Expect others to push back on some of these ideas, but know that this is important, so stand your ground.

- Expect a detox period where your children (and you) feel worse when screens are taken away, but know God made us to be resilient, and this will resolve.

- Talk through rhythms with your spouse—a family has to be on the same page when it comes to the amount of screen time.

- Once you decide your on/off norms, have a conversation with your kids about what those norms are and why you're adopting them.

- For "on" times, try weekly family movie nights, Saturday morning cartoons, one night a week, days when family members are feeling bad/sick.

- For "off" times, try typical car rides, the dinner table, alone in bedrooms.

- Have one room the family gathers in that does not have a TV or computer.

- Consider excluding screens from your sabbath rhythms, or if you exclude them at other times, have them be a special thing you do on the sabbath.

DISCUSS [40 minutes]

Discuss what you just watched by answering the following questions.

1. In the teaching, the point was made that the battle over screentime is not about "are screens okay" or "how much screentime is too much" but about allowing screens to form our and our children's lives. How have you seen this battle take place in your household?

2. *Curation* is the act of intentionally placing limits around what it seen or unseen, experienced or not experienced. (For example, a museum curator determines what visitors see and don't see.) What options do you have when it comes to curating screentime in your home?

3. In setting guidelines on screentime, it is important to remember *rhythms over rules.* Rules are things that we have to keep, while rhythms are more flexible patterns that can be adapted over time. What are some rhythms you could establish for yourself and your family as it relates to when screens can be "on" and when they should be "off"?

4. In setting guidelines on screentime, it is also important to consider *medium over message*. The way we watch our screens can be even more impactful than what we are actually watching. What rhythms could you establish as it relates to discussing how your family is using devices? What age do you think is appropriate for children to have access to devices?

5. A final principle for setting guidelines on screentime is to consider *communal over individual*. Having screens in certain places in the home (like the family room) can actually encourage spending time together as a family. What are some spaces in your home where you know the screens should *not* be? What will you do this week to change this?

Habits for Cultivating Moments of Play

Practicing good habits of play is a way of cultivating a more Christian imagination that foreshadows the kingdom to come.

- If you're a parent who is out of the house each day, think about making half an hour before or after a concentrated time for presence.

- If you're a parent who is with the kids all day, don't feel guilty about not playing with them constantly. But remember that ten focused minutes of engagement or attention each day could go a long way.

- Draw clear distinctions between when you are playing with them and when they need to play alone or with other kids.

- When you decide to play, treat it like work—stay focused and present with your children. Resist the urge to bring along devices.

Things to Consider for Structuring a Family Sabbath

Just as play is an exercise in looking forward to the kingdom to come, so taking a family sabbath day of rest is an exercise in remembering our salvation.

- When do you start? Could you mark the moment?

- What's one thing to stop during sabbath?

- What's one thing to lean into during sabbath?

- How is worship included?

- Should the outdoors be included?

- What's one family activity that is restful for everyone?

- Could you join forces with friends or family?

- Do you need to limit devices on the sabbath?

RESPOND [10 minutes]

In Romans 12:1–2, the apostle Paul encourages followers of Jesus to not "conform to the pattern of this world." The original wording in the Greek calls up the image of being squeezed into a mold. Paul was teaching that the world is constantly trying to form people into its image, which is a problem because we are actually created in the image of *God*. More broadly, Paul is encouraging each of us to make the right choices when it comes to the rhythms of our lives—the choice to make sacrifices when necessary, to worship regularly, and to make spiritual transformation (becoming more like Jesus) a primary goal for our lives each day.

> Therefore, I urge you, brothers and sisters, in view of God's mercy, to offer your bodies as a living sacrifice, holy and pleasing to God—this is your true and proper worship. Do not conform to the pattern of this world, but be transformed by the renewing of your mind. Then you will be able to test and approve what God's will is—his good, pleasing and perfect will.
> *Romans 12:1–2*

What are some ways the world (our culture or society) attempts to squeeze people into the values it deems acceptable? How have you experienced that squeezing?

Paul commands followers of Jesus to be transformed by the renewing of their minds. How should this command influence your decisions regarding screentime in your household?

PRAY [10 minutes]

Conclude this session by affirming your desire to be intentional when it comes to screens and screentime in your home. Also affirm your decision to curate the rhythms of your household by setting limits and making firm choices. Express your desire to be transformed into the likeness of Jesus and ask for wisdom to manage that process for your children to the degree you are able. Afterward, use the space below to write down any requests mentioned so that you and your group members can continue to pray about them in the week ahead.

NAME   **REQUEST**

PERSONAL STUDY

In this session, we looked at habits of the household related to screentime. As technology continues to expand and grow, we continue to feel more pressure to focus on screens throughout the day—literally at just about any moment. This is why choosing to curate screentime in our households is so important, because allowing continual access to screens means allowing continual formation by forces who may not share our values and priorities. As you work through these exercises, be sure to write down your responses to the questions, as you will be given a few minutes to share your insights at the start of the next session if you are doing this study with others. If you are reading *Habits of the Household* alongside this study, first review chapters 4 and 8 before completing the pages that follow.

THE BASICS OF FORMATION

As we discussed in the group section, the battle over screentime is important because it is a battle over "formation." But what does that term *formation* actually mean? How should we understand it? Why is it important to the habits of the household?

One of the basic doctrines of the Christian faith is that each of us is uniquely designed by our Creator. All humans are created in the image of God (see Genesis 1:26), but each person has also been created with a special identity. Each of us is unique and one of a kind. We are personally gifted by God with a specific personality and specific combination of talents that set us apart from everyone else. That's the good news. We are masterpieces!

The bad news is that we aren't born as finished products. Like all living things, we need to grow and mature. The author of Hebrews addressed this truth when he wrote, "Anyone who lives on milk, being still an infant, is not acquainted with the teaching about righteousness. But solid food is for the mature, who by constant use have trained themselves to distinguish good from evil" (Hebrews 5:13–14). We have to move from spiritual "milk" to "solid food."

This is exactly what God does in our lives when we submit to him. He uses the circumstances of our lives to shape us into the women and men he intends us to be. This is formation. We experience it physically as we grow into our adult bodies, we experience it emotionally as we mature, and we experience it spiritually as we become more like Jesus.

1. Use the chart below to identify moments or landmarks that have been especially meaningful in your formation as a unique individual. Remember that these moments can be positive (such as a marriage) or negative (such as the loss of a parent).

TIME PERIOD	MOMENTS THAT SHAPED YOU
Childhood:	
Teenage years:	
Young adulthood:	
In the past ten years:	

2. The ways in which we were formed in our lives play a big role in determining how we manage the formation of our own families. What are you most afraid of for your children in this phase of their lives? How are those fears connected to your own experiences?

> You adulterous people, don't you know that friendship with the world means enmity against God? Therefore, anyone who chooses to be a friend of the world becomes an enemy of God. Or do you think Scripture says without reason that he jealously longs for the spirit he has caused to dwell in us? But he gives us more grace. That is why Scripture says: "God opposes the proud but shows favor to the humble."
>
> *James 4:4–6*

3. What does it mean to have "friendship with the world"? Why do you think James states that is so dangerous in the life of a believer who wants to be formed into Christ's image?

Consider the stakes for a moment. If we do not teach our kids about sex, screens will be happy to do it for us. If we do not teach them categories of good and evil, then screens will be happy to obscure all of them. If we do not teach them that God made them who they are on purpose, man or woman and black or white, then screens will be happy to confuse their understanding of all of these things. If we do not teach them that buying things will not make them happy and that consumption always leaves you hungrier, then screens will teach them that being a consumer is a way to status and satisfaction. If we do not teach them that the world of nature is ferocious and fantastic, something to be stewarded and stunned by, then the world of screens will teach them that looking at pictures of nature is enough. If we do not teach them that silence is a sacred place where God speaks to us, then screens will make sure they never, ever discover it. If we do not teach them that vulnerable and embodied friendship is the heart of the good life, then screens will relentlessly nudge them toward "connecting" and "liking" their way to endemic loneliness.[22]

4. Consider the stakes when it comes to formation. Where do you see opportunities right now to actively and intentionally guide the members of your household? Where do you have an opportunity this week to communicate a key value or priority to someone in your home?

5. As we consider the phenomenon of formation within our households, we have to remember we are still being formed. Even as adults, we have much room to grow. What is one or more goals you are seeking to achieve in your spiritual life within the next year?

FORMATION AND SCREENS

When it comes to something being "formed," we mostly think in terms of a beginning and end. That's certainly true for inanimate objects such as buildings or cars or electronics. Once an iPhone rolls off the assembly line, it gets packaged and sold—the construction phase is over. The same can be true of ideas and memories. Once they are formed, it's hard to change. Even something organic such as a tree seems to reach a stage where it becomes static. Unchanging.

People are different, however. There is nothing static about human beings because we are always growing, always shifting, and always adapting. There is never a phase of a person's life in which he or she is not being formed. This is true of children and senior citizens alike.

This is exactly why building healthy habits around screentime is so important— because screens are *continually* formational. In fact, research has shown that screens function as one of the strongest habit-forming substances we can encounter. According to one report published by the Mayo Clinic, "Excessive screen time can affect a person's mental, social, and physical health. Too much screen time has been linked to obesity, poor sleep or insomnia, behavioral problems (including impulsive actions), loss of social skills, violence, less time for play, eye strain, neck and back problems, anxiety, depression, and difficulties with work or school."[23]

It's quite a list. Anything that comes through our screens has the potential to change how we think, the way we behave, and the person we are becoming. And the longer we are on our screens, the more impact it has on us and our mental and emotional state.

1. Take a moment to think through the battle lines when it comes to your family and screentime. Who wants to use screens, and how often? Where do disagreements or arguments occur most often? What restrictions or routines are currently in place?

2. Think also about the screens currently present or available in your household. Use the chart below to work through the main potential benefits and harms offered by each one.

DEVICE	POTENTIAL BENEFITS	POTENTIAL PROBLEMS
Phones		
Televisions		
Computers		
Gaming devices		
Social media access		
Other		

At the core of being a parent is the idea of setting limits for your children. "Not that close to the street." "That's enough hot chocolate." "It's bedtime." "No more shows." "You can't sleep over if their parents aren't home." "It's time to let someone else have a turn." The list goes on ad infinitum. Sometimes, I reflect with sheer awe on the number of times I say no in a single day. While I strongly encourage figuring out how to redirect attention to something else ("We can't hit your brother with that bat, but we can hit this ball! Look, it's fun!") and affirm the pursuit of better things ("I know chocolate is good, but you don't want a tummy ache later, right?"), when it comes down to it, it's simply a key part of your job description to protect your child from their infinite desire.[24]

3. Think about this statement in terms of placing limits and boundaries around screentime in your household. Use the space below to brainstorm some potential boundaries around the various types of screens in your home. What might healthy limits look like for each one?

DEVICE	WHAT LIMITS COULD LOOK LIKE
Phones	
Televisions	
Computers	
Gaming devices	
Social media	
Other	

4. One of the principles you explored in the group time this week is that communal screen experiences are far more valuable than isolated screen experiences. What are some ways that you can turn individual screens into family fun or bonding experiences?

Setting boundaries for your children is never fun. It is rarely easy, and it always requires a lot of wisdom. On the pain of setting screentime limits, Lauren reminded me, "The cost is for us to bear. It's going to be hard—yes. One of the hardest things you do. They are going to want them—all the time. And even more, you are going to want them all the time, to make your afternoon or your car ride or your morning easier. There is a true loss to a parent's time and capacity. But as parents we take the pain now so our kids don't have to later."[25]

5. When it comes to setting boundaries for screens, parents must be willing to take steps and have conversations that are potentially uncomfortable—even painful. We do so because we believe the benefits are worth that cost. Where do you need to have an uncomfortable conversation this week about screens and screentime?

THE JOY OF PLAY

There's an important question about this issue of screens and screentime that we have not yet addressed: *Why?* In other words, why do so many people—including both children and adults—have such a high desire to spend time in front of a screen? We know that screens are functionally addictive, but what makes them so appealing?

One answer is simply the joy of play. Specifically, screens can offer many different avenues for moving away from the work and drudgery of our everyday lives and step into something completely different: a world of play. This includes games, movies, and television shows. But it also includes puzzles, visual stimulation, connection with friends through conversation, and interaction with the stories and experiences of strangers.

In short, *screens are fun.* This is why they are so tempting—especially to children who are all about play and don't yet understand the costs associated with being on screens all the time. So while it is critical to have boundaries in place so that *fun* doesn't turn into *formation*, it is also important for us to think deeply about the need for play in our lives and in our households. So, we will dig into that topic in greater detail in this personal study.

1. Human beings are created with a need for work and achievement, but we also have a need for play. What are some ways you satisfy that need in your life? What are some of the primary ways that your spouse and your children seek to satisfy that need?

Play is a way to reenchant a disenchanted world.[26] This is serious business. Think about it. A world without play is a world without magic. And a world without magic is a world without resurrection. And in a world without resurrection, nothing good can come true. Which means every fairy tale is a lie. Play, then, is a rebellion against the greatest lie. It is an act of war in allegiance to the greatest truth—that Christ is risen and fairy tales really do come true—namely, the one we're living in. Hallelujah! Let's pause the tasks, then, and play ourselves into Easter people. So it is that to play—I mean to really play—is an exercise of imagining the kingdom, a practice of bearing witness to it right in our own living rooms and back yards.[27]

2. Growing up, what did it mean for you to play? What did that look like in your life, and how did you benefit from those experiences?

3. Consider the following three foundational principles for play in the home. Use the assessments below to evaluate your current experiences with each one.

Principle 1: Habitually Read Imaginative Stories to Your Children: We are all born with this longing for another world, but it is not a given that we will keep it. Our fallen world has a way of dulling our imaginations and training us to accept much less than the glory of the kingdom that

God is building through Jesus and his church. For that reason, we have to see that training and exercising the imagination are as righteous as training and exercising the body or the mind. The primary means of this exercise is story.[28]

In a typical week, how often do you take time to personally read stories with your children?

[Rarely]   [Daily]

Principle 2: Habitually Accept Your Children's Invitation to Play: I think regular play with children is a sign that something in the household is going right. Because it can easily feel like there is always something better to do. My kids ask me fifty times a day to play with them—and that's only a fraction of the requests Lauren gets. Of course, there's always something that seems more urgent—I've got clients waiting on emails and payroll that needs to be run. There's a patch of drywall that needs to be replaced. I have a talk to prepare or a draft chapter to work on. The list is never ending—that's true for all of us, which is why we need rhythms of play with children to remind us that the world doesn't depend on it.[29]

In a typical week, how often do you pretend with your kids or actively join them in a game?

[Rarely]   [Daily]

Principle 3: Habitually Send Them Out to Play on Their Own: No parent can, or should, always accept their children's invitations to play. And we shouldn't feel guilty about that. On the contrary, we should recognize that when we say no to play and send them out on their own, something important is happening. Whether this is sending kids to the back yard or telling your teen to turn off the TV and go take a hike, instructing them to go out and engage with the world on their own means we invite them to get comfortable with the struggle against boredom (which is really just the struggle against the fallen imagination) and do the good work of play by themselves.[30]

In a typical week, how often do your children play in ways that do not involve screens?

1	2	3	4	5	6	7	8	9	10

[Rarely]   [Daily]

4. As we've seen, being proactive in creating plans is helpful for establishing healthy habits and rhythms in our homes. Given this, what are some specific steps that you can take *this week* to more fully incorporate these three principles into your household?

5. One way that play overlaps with the other habits of the household is Sabbath. What can you do to incorporate fun into your weekly rhythm of rest?

CONNECT AND DISCUSS

Take some time today to connect with a fellow group member and discuss some of the key insights from this session. Use any of the following prompts to help guide your discussion.

What felt the most challenging in the material that you've covered in this session? Why?

What questions are you wrestling through when it comes to screens and screentime?

Where do you feel like you've experienced a "win" as a household when it comes to screens?

Talk about the role of healthy play in our lives. What does that look like for your children? What does that look like for you as an adult?

Which suggestions from this week are you planning on trying in your household as it relates to screentime and play? What do you hope to experience?

CATCH UP AND READ AHEAD

Use this time to go back and complete any of the study and reflection questions from previous days that you weren't able to finish. Make a note below of any revelations you've had and reflect on any growth or personal insights you've gained.

Make sure you've read chapters 3 and 9 in *Habits of the Household* before your next group gathering. Use the space below to make note of anything in those chapters that stands out to you or encourages you.

SCHEDULE

WEEK 4

BEFORE GROUP MEETING	Read chapters 3 and 9 in *Habits of the Household* Read the Welcome section (page 93)
GROUP MEETING	Discuss the Connect questions Watch the video teaching for session 4 Discuss the questions that follow as a group Do the closing exercise and pray (pages 93–101)
STUDY 1	Complete the daily study (pages 105–107)
STUDY 2	Complete the daily study (pages 108–110)
STUDY 3	Complete the daily study (pages 111–113)
CONNECT AND DISCUSS	Connect with someone in your group (page 114)
CATCH UP AND READ AHEAD **(BEFORE WEEK 5 GROUP MEETING)**	Read chapters 6 and 7 in *Habits of the Household* Complete any unfinished personal studies (page 115)

HABITS FOR USING DISCIPLINE AS DISCIPLESHIP

Whoever spares the rod hates their children, but the one who loves their children is careful to discipline them.

PROVERBS 13:24

There is a big difference between hurt and harm. We all hurt sometimes in facing hard truths, but it makes us grow. . . . Facing reality is usually not a damaging experience, even though it can hurt.

DR. HENRY CLOUD[31]

All the great temptations appear first in the region of the mind and can be fought and conquered there. We have been given the power to close the door of the mind.

AMY CARMICHAEL[32]

WELCOME [read on your own]

We have already addressed several topics in this study that often make parents uncomfortable: putting kids to bed, leading family devotions, placing limits on screen-entime, and more. Now we are going to address what might be the *most* difficult—and most important—duty that parents must fulfill: disciplining their children when they step out of line.

For most of us, our discomfort with discipline can be traced to our own experiences as children. Maybe our parents were too harsh in their criticism or too tough in their physical punishments. Or maybe our parents were too lax in their supervision or never present long enough in our lives to enforce anything that looked like discipline.

We all carry scars from our childhood and feel apprehensive about passing those scars on to our own kids.

At the same time, our children's need for discipline is evident. We see it every day in the way they think, speak, and behave. They need guidance. They need to be formed. Discipline is a critical element of that formation and a critical piece in making sure our household functions smoothly—even though it is not pleasant for anyone. As we read in Scripture, "No discipline seems pleasant at the time, but painful. Later on, however, it produces a harvest of righteousness and peace for those who have been trained by it" (Hebrews 12:11).

Once again, the power of habits can help us in this regard. Specifically, building healthy habits into our role as disciplinarians is a great way to make sure we keep the focus of discipline where it belongs—on discipleship rather than punishment. In this way, we can be sure that the discipline we are enacting will produce "a harvest of righteousness" in our children.

CONNECT [10 minutes]

Get the session started by choosing one or both of the following questions to discuss together as a group:

- What is something that spoke to your heart in last week's personal study that you would like to share with the group?

—*or*—

- What style of discipline did your parents employ when you were growing up? What feelings do you have about the way they disciplined you?

WATCH [20 minutes]

Now watch the video for this session. Below is an outline of the key points covered during the teaching. Record any key concepts that stand out to you.

Outline

I. Key moments of discipline will always catch us off guard.

    A. The goal of discipline *should* be to bring a struggling heart back to the unconditional love of God.

    B. This can be difficult when we as parents are also imperfect, which is why we need habits.

II. Habit #1: Take a moment to stop and say a quick prayer.

    A. Most moments of discipline don't happen on our terms but are embedded in a crisis.

    B. "Pause prayers" allow us to briefly stop and seek the Savior in those hectic moments.

    C. This reorients us away from what seems like the problem and focuses us on God.

III. Habit #2: Think about what you are communicating through your body language.

    A. It is important to consider what we are communicating before we verbally say anything.

    B. Think about the child's body. How much of what's happening is caused by hunger, tiredness, sickness, or something else that is physical in nature?

    C. Think of your own body. How are you postured and what emotions are you radiating?

IV. Habit #3: Practice liturgies of reconciliation.

    A. Discipline is not finished until there has been reconciliation.

    B. We don't just stop when the misbehavior stops; we need to restore the relationship.

    C. Three steps to move toward reconciliation:

        1. Apology: Help your child practice saying he or she is sorry.

        2. Forgiveness: Words of forgiveness move us out of conflict and into reconciliation.

        3. Action: Act out reconciliation physically, such as by giving your child a hug.

Notes

Pause Prayers

The beauty of pause prayers is that they are short prayers you can bring into any moment.

- When you're interrupted by your child's behavior: Lord, remind me that shepherding my child, not efficiency, is the goal of parenting. Help me to make time for this and not want to rush through this moment.

- When you feel like your children are acting up on purpose to ruin your day: Lord, remind me that my children are not out to get me, they are just children, and when I was in sin you came to me in love, not anger.

- When you seriously feel that you just can't take it anymore: Lord, remind me that at the end of myself, I find more of you. Be my strength here.

- When you're not sure how to discipline your child: Lord, please give me the wisdom in this situation that only you can impart. Guide me in this moment.

- When you are not sure whether to be firm or gentle: "Lord, remind me that you parent me with both grace and truth. Help me to be like you in this moment."

- When you're feeling sick of them: "Lord, help me to remember I am more like this child than not. And you parent me with gentleness."

- When it's an emergency or you just can't think of anything else: "Lord, help!" (Remember, Ann Lamott once wrote that the most essential three prayers are "Help!" and "Thanks!" and Wow!")

DISCUSS [40 minutes]

Discuss what you just watched by answering the following questions.

1. Key moments of discipline will always catch us off guard because we are reacting to actions from our children that we did not expect. Given this, why is it important to have a strategy for turning discipline into discipleship *before* these out-of-the-blue moments arrive?

2. The goal of discipline should be to bring a struggling heart back to the unconditional love of Jesus. When have you seen that kind of discipline accomplished well?

3. The theme of this session is that we as parents can reframe moments of discipline—what feels like punishment—into moments of discipleship for our children. In your own words, how would you describe the difference between those two ideas?

4. In video teaching, we looked at three healthy habits that parents can use when discipline is necessary: pause prayers, body language, and liturgies of reconciliation. Which of those three are you most interested in trying yourself? Why?

5. Reconciliation is something that's easy to forget during moments of discipline—restoring the relationship and bringing the wanderer back into fellowship. What might it look like for you to emphasize reconciliation in your household as part of the discipline process?

Habits of Conversation

Conversation turns family into friends and friends into family. We begin teaching habits of friendship by teaching habits of conversation. Here are some starter questions:

- What was the best and worst part of today? Anything you laughed at?

- Did anyone get in trouble today?

- Does anyone in your class not have a friend?

- What did you think about before you fell asleep last night?

- Who do you like sitting by in class? Who do you not want to sit by?

- What's your favorite thing to do with Mom/Dad/brother/sister/friend?

- Who is your best friend right now? Anyone you're mad at?

- What do you think you're really good at? Bad at?

- What is the bravest thing you've done?

- Is there anything you want to tell me or ask me about?

- Is there anything you notice about the world that you think other people don't notice?

- What do you pray about when you talk to God? When do you pray?

RESPOND [10 minutes]

The book of Hebrews was written to Jewish followers of Jesus who were experiencing hardships because of their faith. In the early days of the church, following Jesus often brought real consequences—such as excommunication from the temple or synagogues, rejection from family, imprisonment, and even death. In Hebrews 11, the author reminds his readers of the "great cloud of witnesses" who have gone before them—prophets and patriarchs who endured hardships even as they paved the way. Then, in Hebrews 12, he reminds his readers that God often uses hardship as a method of discipline—not to punish us, but as part of our discipleship.

> Endure hardship as discipline; God is treating you as his children. For what children are not disciplined by their father? If you are not disciplined— and everyone undergoes discipline—then you are not legitimate, not true sons and daughters at all. Moreover, we have all had human fathers who disciplined us and we respected them for it. How much more should we submit to the Father of spirits and live! They disciplined us for a little while as they thought best; but God disciplines us for our good, in order that we may share in his holiness. No discipline seems pleasant at the time, but painful. Later on, however, it produces a harvest of righteousness and peace for those who have been trained by it.
>
> *Hebrews 12:7–11*

How do these verses reinforce the connection between discipline and discipleship?

What does it mean for us to submit to discipline from our heavenly Father?

PRAY [10 minutes]

Conclude this session by praying together about these topics of discipline and discipleship. Remember God's promise to give us wisdom whenever we ask for it (see James 1:5) and be sure to ask for wisdom in your specific circumstances. Pray also for eyes to see specific opportunities in the coming weeks to elevate the experience of discipline in your household. Afterward, use the space below to write down any requests mentioned so that you and your group members can continue to pray about them in the week ahead.

NAME   **REQUEST**

SESSION FOUR

PERSONAL STUDY

Being part of a household brings a lot of privileges. Of course, privileges are always accompanied by responsibilities. We feel the weight of those responsibilities as parents as we navigate mornings and evenings, mealtimes, screentime, and more. We willingly carry so much responsibility for our children because our love for them is so deep. It's because of those two realities—the balance between privilege and responsibility—that habits are a powerful tool. They help us savor the former and succeed in the latter . . . including the critical responsibility of *discipline*. As you work through the exercises in this personal study section, be sure to write down your responses to the questions, as you will be given a few minutes to share your insights at the start of the next session if you are doing this study with others. If you are reading *Habits of the Household* alongside this study, first review chapters 3 and 9.

A DEEPER LOOK AT DISCIPLESHIP

We made the case during this week's group time that we, as parents, should approach discipline within our households not as punishment but as a form of discipleship. But this begs the questions: *What is discipleship? What does discipleship look like on a practical level?*

At its most basic level, discipleship is the process of a follower (a disciple) learning to think and behave like a teacher. In the rabbinical tradition of Jesus' day, a disciple literally "did life" with his teacher—he walked where his teacher walked, assisted whenever the teacher taught, learned to value what the teacher valued, did whatever the teacher did, and ultimately strove to become as much like the teacher as possible. Eventually, the goal of a disciple was to become a teacher himself and begin the process all over again by training new disciples.

It's easy to see the connection between discipleship and parenting. As parents, we "do life" with our children. We teach them our values and priorities. We show them not only how to live and grow but also how to live and grow in ways that reflect our own lives. We are training our children to become like us. Christianity adds another level to this process because, even as we strive to follow Jesus as adults and become the people he created us to be, we also encourage our children to follow our example so they can become everything God intends for them to be. (This is the concept of *formation* we discussed in a previous session.)

Seen through the lens of discipleship, the moments where discipline is required in our households are no longer chores or hardships that need to be endured. Instead, they become opportunities for us to teach and lead in ways that bring a significant return.

1. What are some seasons or moments from your past in which you experienced discipleship in a meaningful way? What lessons did you carry into your life from those seasons?

2. Think of your relationship with your children in terms of that teacher-disciple model. You are the teacher, and your children are the disciples. In what ways is that process currently going well? Where do you see room for improvement in that relationship?

Then Jesus came to them and said, "All authority in heaven and on earth has been given to me. Therefore go and make disciples of all nations, baptizing them in the name of the Father and of the Son and of the Holy Spirit, and teaching them to obey everything I have commanded you. And surely I am with you always, to the very end of the age."

Matthew 28:18–20

3. Jesus' "great commission" to his disciples gives us a picture of what he expects from us as his disciples. Where do you see connections between Jesus' commission to his disciples and your role as a parent within your household? Explain your response.

God's response to our misbehavior is to love us back into relationship, no matter the personal cost to him. Picture it like this: the biblical movement of discipline begins in love (creation), moves through human misbehavior (fall), continues through God's sacrifice in response to that misbehavior (redemption), and then calls us to action and ends in love and reconciliation again (consummation).

The plotline of the story of God is entirely shaped by the discipline of God, and that is a good thing, because that means it takes the shape of his love. Hebrews sums it up perfectly: "the Lord disciplines the one he loves" (Hebrews 12:6).

And this loving discipline of the heavenly father is what creates disciples who in turn love others like he loved us (see John 13:34). You do not need a degree in linguistics to see the root connection between discipline and discipleship. God's discipline is the process that creates God's disciples.[33]

4. What are some ways you have felt God's discipline throughout your journey as a disciple? When has he stepped in to correct you and guide you in ways that were meaningful?

5. Think about a recent experience in which you needed to step in and discipline your child. With the benefit of hindsight, what went well during that experience? Where do you now see opportunities to make those moments of discipline moments of discipleship as well?

A DEEPER LOOK AT DISCIPLINE

Viewing discipline through the lens of discipleship does not mean that we, as parents, ignore the seriousness of our children's wrongdoing and rebellious behavior. Nor does it mean that we abandon the reality of consequences for our children's wrongful actions. In fact, the opposite is true. Because discipline is a part of discipleship, feeling the sting of negative consequences is vitally important. That sting helps us learn important lessons and make necessary changes.

Just consider some of the ways that God disciplined his children throughout the Bible. When Adam and Eve disobeyed the Lord by eating from the tree of the knowledge of good and evil, he banished them from the Garden of Eden (see Genesis 3:23). During the time of the exodus, when Aaron's sons Nadab and Abihu made a mockery of their role as priests, they were struck down by the fire of God (see Leviticus 10:1–2). When Moses ignored a command from God, he was denied entry into the Promised Land (see Numbers 20:12). When David committed adultery and murder, he was forced to deal with "the sword" within his own household (see 2 Samuel 12:10). And when the Israelites rejected God as a community for generations, they were removed from the promised land through war and exile (see Jeremiah 25:8–14).

As parents, we must not abandon the reality of consequences. At the same time, we must wrestle with the reality that our instincts are often incorrect. Instead of using discipline as a means for discipleship, we settle for punishment as a means of control. This is why healthy habits of the household are critical for everyone involved.

1. One way to increase the effectiveness of discipline is to make sure everyone is aware of potential consequences *before* that discipline becomes necessary. As an exercise, what would the consequences be if a child in your home was guilty of the following?

STARTING A FIGHT WITH A SIBLING	
DIRECTLY DISOBEYING YOU	
USING PROFANITY	
STEALING MONEY IN THE HOME	

If discipline were easy, we wouldn't need to talk about practicing habits to guide us. We would just spontaneously respond with the right reaction. When a small child is about to run out into a street, for example, our instinct is the same every time, and it is always right—grab them. Protect them. It is simple, and it is never wrong. But discipline is not the same—not at all.

We need habits that help us practice discipline as discipleship because, frankly, we have all the wrong instincts. Discipline never happens at a moment of convenience. We are always too tired, or running late, or pulled in different directions, or something else. Even worse, depending on your upbringing and the harm that may have been done to you under the guise of discipline, you may carry an awful lot of awful baggage into these moments.[34]

2. We need *habits* to help us practice discipline as discipleship because we all have the wrong instincts. Think about the last time you disciplined your child. What factors (like being tired, running late, being pulled in different directions) impacted that discipline?

3. Depending on your upbringing and the harm done to you under the guise of discipline, you may carry that kind of baggage into your moments of discipline. Do you think that is a factor in your discipline? What kind of baggage might you be bringing into a situation?

> By nature, discipline happens in the moments when we are not prepared for it. When you planned the shopping outing on the way to the park, you did not plan for the twenty-minute meltdown in the aisle or the fight over bringing a snack onto the playground. This is the reality of discipline. It happens on the move, but it does not have to be off the cuff. Habits of pausing help with that.[35]

4. Think about this idea of pausing in the middle of a discipline opportunity—and especially pausing for a brief prayer—before you discipline. What are some practical steps you can take to remember that "pause prayer" when you are actively in the middle of parenting?

5. Reconciliation is an important element of discipline and discipleship. What habits or rituals can you use to welcome a child back into good standing once the discipline is over?

THE IMPORTANCE OF CONVERSATION

Throughout this exploration of habits within our households, we have focused on some of the most basic rhythms of human life: waking up, falling asleep, eating a meal, watching a movie, correcting a misbehavior, and more. As we continue this theme of discipline and discipleship, there is one more rhythm that becomes critically important: *conversation*.

In many ways, conversation serves as the foundation for our relationships. This is true of our relationships with friends and family—the people we love and trust the most in this world. And it is also true of our relationship with our heavenly Father. Conversation is how we learn to know and be known. It is the primary way we experience connection with others.

For that reason, conversation is critical within our households. It's how we laugh together, share opinions, make memories, tell stories, and so on. It's how we function as a family and grow into friends. Importantly, conversation is also a critical element of discipline. The way we speak to each other before, during, and after the intense experiences of correction and reconciliation is a vital part of that process. Healthy conversation is required for healthy discipline—especially when we rightly understand discipline as discipleship.

1. In general, how would you describe the level of conversation within your household, starting with the conversations between yourself and your children? What about the conversations that your children have with each other?

2. When it comes to the quality of conversations, *when* can be an important factor. How open and talkative are your children at different times during the day? (If you have multiple children, make a separate mark for each one on the assessments below.)

How receptive are your children to opportunities for conversation when they first wake up?

| 1 | 2 | 3 | 4 | 5 | 6 | 7 | 8 | 9 | 10 |

[Not receptive]   [Very receptive]

How receptive are your children for conversation after school?

| 1 | 2 | 3 | 4 | 5 | 6 | 7 | 8 | 9 | 10 |

[Not receptive]   [Very receptive]

How receptive are your children for conversation at mealtimes?

| 1 | 2 | 3 | 4 | 5 | 6 | 7 | 8 | 9 | 10 |

[Not receptive]   [Very receptive]

How receptive are your children for conversation on car rides?

| 1 | 2 | 3 | 4 | 5 | 6 | 7 | 8 | 9 | 10 |

[Not receptive]   [Very receptive]

How receptive are your children for conversation before bedtime?

| 1 | 2 | 3 | 4 | 5 | 6 | 7 | 8 | 9 | 10 |

[Not receptive]   [Very receptive]

3. Body language is an important part of conversation, but especially during moments of discipline. What are some practical steps you can take to manage your body language—and be aware of your child's body language—during times of correction and reconciliation?

> One of the unique opportunities of a parent is to use conversation to walk your child through their mess. But vulnerability is not a given, and usually a child is honest because a parent is honest first. A child is vulnerable because a parent demonstrates it. A child engages in conversation because a parent seeks them out.
>
> This is the great burden and blessing of parenting—we have the opportunity and the duty to seek out our children and use conversation to help heal the pain that we all carry. Trauma and secrets can burn us up from the inside out, but conversation is what turns those destructive fires of our own fallenness into the refining fire of God's grace. And so often it comes through the grace of conversation.[36]

4. What would it look like for you to intentionally be vulnerable with your children this week? What would be appropriate for you to share and discuss based on their ages and maturity?

5. Which habits of conversation will you try in your home this week? What are some other ways you can incorporate conversation into the process of discipline and correction?

CONNECT AND DISCUSS

Take some time today to connect with a fellow group member and discuss some of the key insights from this session. Use any of the following prompts to help guide your discussion.

What new habits from this study have you put into practice in your home? What is working?

Parents should view discipline as an opportunity for discipleship, not punishment. How would you explain that idea to someone who had never heard it before?

Which habits related to discipline do you want to implement this week? Why those habits?

Where and when do you see conversations taking place at a deeper level within your home? How would you like to see conversations among your family improve or grow?

What has inspired or challenged you the most up to this point in the study? Why?

CATCH UP AND READ AHEAD

Use this time to go back and complete any of the study and reflection questions from previous days that you weren't able to finish. Make a note below of any revelations you've had and reflect on any growth or personal insights you've gained.

Make sure you've read chapters 6 and 7 in *Habits of the Household*. Use the space below to make note of anything in the chapters that stands out to you or encourages you.

SCHEDULE
WEEK 5

BEFORE GROUP MEETING	Read chapters 6 and 7 in *Habits of the Household* Read the Welcome section (page 119)
GROUP MEETING	Discuss the Connect questions Watch the video teaching for session 5 Discuss the questions that follow as a group Do the closing exercise and pray (pages 119–127)
PERSONAL STUDY 1	Complete the daily study (pages 131–133)
PERSONAL STUDY 2	Complete the daily study (pages 134–136)
PERSONAL STUDY 3	Complete the daily study (pages 137–141)
CONNECT AND DISCUSS	Connect with someone in your group (page 142)
WRAP IT UP	Complete any unfinished personal studies (page 143) Discuss the next study you want to go through together

SESSION FIVE

HABITS TO HELP YOU IMAGINE THE FUTURE

If people can't see what God is doing, they stumble all over themselves; but when they attend to what he reveals, they are most blessed.

PROVERBS 29:18 MSG

The world becomes stranger, the pattern more complicated. . . . Not the intense moment isolated, with no before and after, but a lifetime burning in every moment.

T. S. ELIOT[37]

It is the joy of work well done that enables us to enjoy rest, just as it is the experiences of hunger and thirst that make food and drink such pleasures.

ELISABETH ELLIOT[38]

WELCOME [read on your own]

As we have seen throughout this study, our lives are filled with habits and routines. Sometimes it seems as if our days are overflowing with them! Morning routines. School routines. Work routines. Mealtime routines. Cleanup routines. Evening routines. Bedtime routines. Then back to the morning routines as we start all over again.

It's not just individual days that can feel like a spin cycle of sameness. Each week has its own rhythm and flow. Mondays are Mondays—nobody's favorite. Many of us have rhythms of church on Wednesdays or Sundays or both. We have sports practices and games. We have date nights and late work nights. As Thursday rolls around, we all start getting excited for the weekend, which has its own rhythms and routines. Then we're back to Monday again.

Weeks flow into months. Months flow into years. And somehow, by some unimaginable calculus, years flow into generations in a way that is both incredibly slow and unbelievably fast. If we are not careful, the rhythms of our lives can wax and wane until we find ourselves standing at the door of our empty nest and asking, "How did I get here?"

This is why we are going to conclude this study by breaking out of all the rhythms that we have discussed in the previous sessions. We are going to end our study by looking not to today, or to next week, or even to the next few months, but to a more distant future. Specifically, we're going to get a sneak preview of our legacy as leaders of our households.

CONNECT [10 minutes]

Get the session started by choosing one or both of the following questions to discuss together as a group:

- What insights did you glean from last week's personal study? How has this study overall changed the way you think about your habits?

—or—

- People with grown children often say, "Cherish it now, because they grow up so quickly." When have you recently been struck by that reality?

WATCH [20 minutes]

Now watch the video for this session. Below is an outline of the key points covered during the teaching. Record any key concepts that stand out to you.

Outline

I. As parents, we need to "look up" at times and consider the big picture as it relates to our kids.

    A. Parenting is "the longest shortest time," and in that paradox, we need God's perspective.

    B. To keep our hearts alive, we need to see the future how God sees it (see Proverbs 29:18).

    C. God has called us during this limited time to parent these little image bearers we call children.

II. Take a moment to fill out an age chart for your household (see page xx).

    A. Write your name and age and your spouse's name and age in the left-hand column.

    B. Write the names of your children and their ages in the columns to the right.

    C. Notice the *ages* and *stages* and write down some notes in the margins.

III. Now reflect on your age chart using a tried-and-true spiritual practice called *examen*.

    A. Meditate on your past and your family's past and consider these questions:

        1. What I am I grateful for?

        2. Where was God present during those times?

        3. Where do I still need God's grace and forgiveness?

    B. Meditate on your future and your family's future and consider these questions:

        1. What am I hopeful for?

        2. Where do I feel like I need help?

        3. What am I scared of?

IV. Now reflect on what God might be teaching you in each stage as a family.

    A. Newborn years: times where parenting is at is most physical and demanding.

    B. Early formation years: times with toddlers and young children in the home.

    C. In-between years: times between the toddler and adolescent years.

    D. Adolescent years: challenging times with incredible breakthroughs and difficult arguments.

V. The end of habits of the household is the beginning of the rest of your life.

    A. The goal is not performing perfectly as parents but seeing God as the ultimate parent.

    B. As we become God's children, we all become brothers and sisters in his kingdom.

Notes

AGE CHART FOR YOUR HOUSEHOLD

	YOU: _____ SPOUSE: _____	CHILD: _____	CHILD: _____	CHILD: _____	CHILD: _____	CHILD: _____
Age now:						
5 years:						
10 years:						
15 years:						
20 years:						
25 years:						
30 years:						
35 years:						
40 years:						

EXAMEN PRACTICE FOR LIFE STAGES

STAGE	PAST	FUTURE
Newborn	What am I grateful for in this stage? Where was God present in this stage? Where do I need God's grace and forgiveness as I reflect on this time?	What am I hopeful for in this stage? What do I need help with in this stage? What scares me about this stage?
EARLY FORMATION	What am I grateful for in this stage? Where was God present in this stage? Where do I need God's grace and forgiveness as I reflect on this time?	What am I hopeful for in this stage? What do I need help with in this stage? What scares me about this stage?
IN-BETWEEN	What am I grateful for in this stage? Where was God present in this stage? Where do I need God's grace and forgiveness as I reflect on this time?	What am I hopeful for in this stage? What do I need help with in this stage? What scares me about this stage?
ADOLESCENT	What am I grateful for in this stage? Where was God present in this stage? Where do I need God's grace and forgiveness as I reflect on this time?	What am I hopeful for in this stage? What do I need help with in this stage? What scares me about this stage?

DISCUSS [40 minutes]

Discuss what you just watched by answering the following questions.

1. The newborn years are significant for every parent. If you have been through that stage, how did you change as a person during those years? How did you change as a child of God? If you have not yet been through that stage, what are you most looking forward to about this time in your family's life? What scares you the most about this stage?

2. The early formation years are times of innocence but also the beginnings of disobedience. If you have been through that stage, what traits did you notice that your children shared with you? What fruit of the Spirit did you see in them? If you have not yet been through this stage, which of your traits would you like to see and not see in your children?

3. The in-between years are times of education and formation. If you have been through that stage, what experiences did you share with your children that stand out the most to you? How has God used or redeemed that stage in your family's life? If you have not yet been through this stage, what are some ways that you could steward this time and implement some habits of the household? How will you be present with your kids during this time?

4. Raising teenagers can be a difficult experience, especially in a world that insists on molding them through technology. If you have been through that stage, what do you feel you navigated well and not-so-well? How did God reveal his grace to you during this time? If you have not yet been through this stage, what concerns you the most when you consider that your child will be an adolescent? What kind of parent do you want to be at this stage?

5. Think about that season when your children mature into adults and even into parents of their own households. What will "success" look like for you in that season? What are your biggest goals to get there? What will you do *now* to start moving toward those goals?

RESPOND [10 minutes]

The book of Ecclesiastes is a haunting collection of wisdom that scholars believe was penned by King Solomon. The primary theme is that Solomon dipped his toe into every area of life that society considers important—money, fame, knowledge, power, the arts, romance, and more. He lived life to the fullest, yet he found everything meaningless without God. Ecclesiastes 12 contains Solomon's reflections on aging. He concludes that we should seek God and seek to make a difference in this world while we are young, before the trials of old age wear us down. As you read these verses, note the imagery Solomon uses to represent the facets of old age:

> Remember your Creator
> in the days of your youth,
> before the days of trouble come
> and the years approach when you will say,
> "I find no pleasure in them"—
> before the sun and the light
> and the moon and the stars grow dark,
> and the clouds return after the rain;
> when the keepers of the house tremble,
> and the strong men stoop,
> when the grinders cease because they are few,
> and those looking through the windows grow dim;
> when the doors to the street are closed
> and the sound of grinding fades;
> when people rise up at the sound of birds,
> but all their songs grow faint;
> when people are afraid of heights
> and of dangers in the streets;
> when the almond tree blossoms
> and the grasshopper drags itself along
> and desire no longer is stirred.
> Then people go to their eternal home
> and mourners go about the streets.
>
> Remember him—before the silver cord is severed,
> and the golden bowl is broken;
> before the pitcher is shattered at the spring,

and the wheel broken at the well,
    and the dust returns to the ground it came from,
        and the spirit returns to God who gave it.

Ecclesiastes 12:1–7

As you think about what your family will experience over the next few years, what guiding principles do you want to "remember"? What are the major priorities you want to keep hold of?

As a parent, you have a tremendous opportunity to influence lives right now. What is one thing you have learned in this study that will help you take advantage of that opportunity?

PRAY [10 minutes]

Conclude this session by acknowledging your life, and the lives of your children, are held firmly in your heavenly Father's hands. Ask to receive God's blessings in your home over the next five years, ten years, twenty years, and more. Ask also that God would continue to provide the wisdom you need to be an effective steward of the children that the Lord has entrusted to your care. Afterward, use the space below to write down any requests mentioned so that you and your group members can continue to pray about them in the weeks ahead.

NAME   **REQUEST**

_____   _____

_____   _____

_____   _____

_____   _____

_____   _____

_____   _____

PERSONAL STUDY

The topics that we have covered in this study are critical for your family—the rhythms of waking and sleeping, eating and learning, setting boundaries and offering correction. You have the opportunity right now to harness the power of healthy habits for the benefit of yourself and those you love the most. However, implementing those habits will produce dividends beyond just your current moment. The work you invest today in yourself and your children will pay off not only for years to come but also for generations. These habits can bless you, your children, your children's children, and beyond. Don't lose sight of that reality as this study comes to a close. Stay focused and stay faithful! The rewards are worth it. Keep this in minds as you work through these exercises, and be sure to continue to record your responses to the questions. If you are reading *Habits of the Household* alongside this study, first review chapters 6 and 7.

REFLECTING ON THE FUTURE

As mentioned in the group time, it's easy to get lost in the trenches of parenting every day. As moms and dads, we tend to keep our heads down and focus on the moment—what our family needs in the next five minutes or five hours. Anything beyond that is often difficult to predict.

Yet it is also valuable to take a step back from time to time and focus on where we are going. This includes our long-term goals as a family, but it also includes the trajectories of each child as an individual. It's important to think about what your children need now, but it's also important to think about and plan for what they will need in the future.

This idea is not only practical but also biblical. As previously noted, Moses commanded the Israelites to teach God's laws to their children so they would not forget what the Lord had done (see Deuteronomy 6:12). The psalmist Asaph wrote, "We will not hide [God's teachings] from their descendants; we will tell the next generation the praiseworthy deeds of the Lord, his power, and the wonders he has done" (Psalm 78:4). King David wrote, "One generation commends your works to another; they tell of your mighty acts" (Psalm 145:4).

It is an important exercise to reflect on the future from time to time. You began this type of thinking with the age chart exercise that you completed during this week's group study time. Now, keep it going by thinking through the following critical questions.

1. Take a moment to assess the current strengths of your children. What do they do well? How might those strengths benefit your children as they mature into adulthood? Use the space below to answer those questions for each of your children.

MY CHILD'S CURRENT STRENGTHS	HOW THEY WILL BENEFIT HIM/HER IN THE FUTURE

2. Next, take a moment to think objectively about the current weaknesses of your children. Where do they struggle? What skills or character traits do they lack? And, importantly, how might those weaknesses impact them as they grow into adults?

MY CHILD'S CURRENT WEAKNESSES	HOW THEY WILL IMPACT HIM/HER IN THE FUTURE

3. Considering the different healthy habits you have explored throughout this study, which ones have the most potential for maximizing your children's strengths? How will you incorporate those particular habits into your home?

4. Which habits or routines have the most potential for helping your children grapple with their weaknesses and grow? How will you incorporate those habits into your home?

5. During the group time, you talked about what success might look like for your family five, ten, twenty, even forty years from now. Use the space below to dig deeper into that concept. What are five goals you would like your family to achieve in the next ten years? Be specific about what each of those goals would entail and who will achieve them.

Goal #1: ....

Goal #2: ....

Goal #3: ....

Goal #4: ....

Goal #5: ....

REFLECTING ON MARRIAGE

We have spent most of our time in this study exploring the habits of the household based on the relationships between parents and children. Those relationships have a tendency to dominate our homes. Parents naturally think about their children before themselves, which often means the rhythms and routines within a household are focused on its smallest occupants.

But there is also much to be gained by exploring the vital connection between husband and wife. For one thing, it is naïve to believe that our connection as parents has no influence on our children. We will struggle deeply to be good parents if we are not first good spouses, and there is nothing that can damage a home quite like strife between Mom and Dad.

On a deeper level, investing in marriage is critical because we are raising our children not only to become adults but also to likely become parents of their own. Our young boys will one day be husbands, and our young girls will one day be wives. How they function in those roles—including the habits they establish in their own households—will be hugely influenced by what they have observed throughout their lives from their own mother and father.

For those reasons and more, we will spend some time in this personal study contemplating marriage in the context of the habits, rhythms, and routines that define our homes. We will also keep an eye on the future as we do so.

1. How would you describe your marriage today? How does your current relationship compare and contrast with what you expected when you first said, "I do"?

2. Think about the rhythms and routines of your household—the stuff you do every day. Which of those rhythms or habits are healthy for your marriage? Which are harmful?

> As a practice, date night is simple enough. You set aside an evening for each other somewhere in the week (whether in or out of the house) and you stick to it. You know you will be too busy and too tired, but that's why you schedule it.
>
> Maybe you watch a movie, or maybe you schedule an evening out. Maybe you cook together or maybe you read to each other. Perhaps you take a walk or you sit down with a glass of wine. Whatever you do, you must know that it will go wrong as often as it goes right. You hoped for conversation, but you're fighting instead. You had great dinner reservations, but the kids got sick. You ordered takeout, but one of you is mad because it blew the budget. You hoped for something romantic, but as it turns out, he keeps checking the score or she keeps checking her phone.
>
> It is never quite the way it was supposed to be. But you try anyway. Because that's not just the story of date night, that's the story of marriage. Sinners trying to love each other never turns out like we thought, but we keep going because we made a covenant. In this sense, the seemingly simple pattern of weekly date night is something much more powerful: it is a way of rehearsing that covenant.[39]

3. In the past month, what experiences have you had with your spouse that could count as "dates"? What do you enjoy most about those experiences?

One of my favorite things to do with Lauren . . . is to ask what she is thinking about for the future and to tell her what I'm thinking about. There is a range of questions here. What friend does she wish she were closer to? What is she hoping for in returning to work? What is broken that we need to fix in our patterns? What is a goal she is hoping for or working toward? Where does she feel our family is headed? What can we do about that? Hopefully, I'll respond with mine or she'll ask too.[40]

4. Think about this habit of dreaming with your spouse and thinking about the future. What might it look like to incorporate something similar into your marriage?

5. We've spent a lot of time in this session thinking about the future, so do the same with your marriage. What are some goals for the relationship over the next year? The next five years?

REFLECTING ON WORK

Parenting and marriage are important rhythms in our household that have a big impact on our children. But another important rhythm is work. The way we approach work influences not only how much time we spend with our children—and how much energy we have left over for them—but also how they will approach their own experiences with work as they grow.

One thing we don't often think about in connection with work is God himself . . . though we should. After all, God is always at work! He poured himself into the work of creation. After the fall of Adam and Eve, he continued to pour himself into the work of redemption and restoration. He works to maintain his relationship with us—to teach us and guide us. And he works as the sovereign Lord of all things throughout the universe, including heaven and earth.

We are also blessed with the opportunity for different kinds of work—though, to be sure, work doesn't often seem like a blessing. Perhaps that's because most of us define work in terms of our *vocation*. Yet that is really just the tip of the iceberg. Our work includes everything we do as stewards not only of our families but also of the earth—of our communities, our cities, and our world. So let's take a deeper look in this personal study at the rhythm of work and at the healthy habits that can ensure our work is a blessing for our households, not a curse.

1. As mentioned above, each of us is engaged every day with different types of work. What are some of the main responsibilities or expectations you carry out as part of your "work"?

2. What lessons did you learn about work from your mother and father? How did their approach to their work shape your own ideas about your work?

> If [children] are going to learn work, *they need to be regularly invited into the work of the house.* This is inevitably messier than it is helpful, at least at first. But how else will they come to understand the satisfaction of a job well done? How will they come to understand the dignity of the work a stay-at-home parent performs? The reason I insist on inviting the boys (or put bluntly, forcing them) into the work of the house is to pull back the curtains and show them that creating a place of hospitality, health, and conversation takes a whole lot of work.[41]

3. One of the best ways for children to learn about work is to be included in the work occurring in and around their household. What are some ways your children are currently participating in the work of your household? Where might there be additional opportunities to invite them to participate more fully or more often?

4. The reality is that work life and home life are often at odds—competing for our energy, time, and attention. This is why it is important to strike a work-life/home-life balance. Use the following questions to evaluate how you are currently doing in maintaining this balance.

How satisfied do you feel about the amount of time you spend with your family in a week?

1	2	3	4	5	6	7	8	9	10

[Unsatisfied]   [Satisfied]

How well do you transition from work life to home life each day?

1	2	3	4	5	6	7	8	9	10

[Poorly]   [Well]

How often do you invite your children to participate in your work or to talk about your vocation?

1	2	3	4	5	6	7	8	9	10

[Rarely]   [Regularly]

How often do you observe a Sabbath each week—a rest from work?

1	2	3	4	5	6	7	8	9	10

[Never]   [Regularly]

Habits for Inviting Children into the Work of the Household:

- Talk about the housework in a way that dignifies the work that is done there.

- If a child can do it for themselves, try your best not to do it for them.

- Teach them tasks as early as possible, whether picking up toys, hammering a nail, taking out trash, washing a dish, folding towels, wiping tables, or sweeping floors.

- Let them help host by greeting guests at the door and offering drinks or snacks, and then helping with clean-up after.

- Let them help you (even when it slows you down)—this may require adding margin in your life so that your housework is not always about maximizing efficiency.

- Work toward an age-appropriate chore system. Let them tangibly check things off and earn rewards, whether money or stickers or something else.[42]

5. Which of those habits could fit well in your routine? What is another habit you could incorporate into your home to help introduce your children to the importance of work?

CONNECT AND DISCUSS

Take some time today to connect with a fellow group member and discuss some of the key insights from this session. Use any of the following prompts to help guide your discussion.

This week's personal study focused on the future, marriage, and work. Which of those topics was most engaging for you? Why?

If comfortable, share some of the goals for your family that you wrote down at the end of Study 1. Which goal feels most important? Which feels most difficult to achieve?

Now that you've been reading and studying about "habits of the household" for several weeks, how has your thinking changed about the rhythms and routines of your home?

What have you enjoyed most throughout this study? Why?

When have you felt convicted or inspired to make a change? What are you planning to add or subtract from your household because of those feelings?

WRAP IT UP

Use this time to go back and complete any of the study and reflection questions from previous days that you weren't able to finish. Make note of what God has revealed to you in these days. Finally, talk with your group about what study you may want to go through next. Put a date on the calendar for when you'll meet next to study God's Word and dive deeper into community.

LEADER'S GUIDE

Thank you for your willingness to lead your group through this study! What you have chosen to do is valuable and will make a great difference in the lives of others. The rewards of being a leader are different from those of participating, and we hope that as you lead you will find your own journey with Christ deepened by this experience.

Habits of the Household is a five-session Bible study built around video content and small-group interaction. As the group leader, imagine yourself as the host of a party. Your job is to take care of your guests by managing the details so that when your guests arrive, they can focus on one another and on the interaction around the topic for that session.

Your role as the group leader is not to answer all the questions or reteach the content—the video, book, and study guide will take care of most of that. Your job is to guide the experience and cultivate your small group into a connected and engaged community. This will make it a place for members to process, question, and reflect.

There are several elements in this leader's guide that will help you as you structure your study and reflection time, so be sure to follow along and take advantage of each one.

BEFORE YOU BEGIN

Before your first meeting, make sure the group members have a copy of this study guide. Alternately, you can hand out the study guides at your first meeting and give the members some time to look over the material and ask any preliminary questions. Also make sure they are aware that they have access to the streaming videos at any time. During your first meeting, ask each member to provide their name, phone number, and email address so you can keep in touch with them.

Generally, the ideal size for a group is eight to ten people, which will ensure that everyone has enough time to participate in discussions. If you have more people, you might want to break up the main group into smaller subgroups. Encourage those who show up at the first meeting to commit to attending the duration of the study, as this will help the group members get to know one another, create stability for the group, and help you know how to best prepare to lead them through the material.

Each of the sessions begins with an opening reflection in the Welcome section. The questions that follow in the Connect section serve as an icebreaker to get the group members thinking about the topic. Some people may want to tell a long story in response to one of these questions, but the goal is to keep the answers brief. Ideally, you want everyone in the group to get a chance to answer, so try to keep the responses to a minute or less. If you have talkative group members, say up front that everyone needs to be brief so everyone has time to share.

Give the group members a chance to answer, but also tell them to feel free to pass if they wish. With the rest of the study, it's generally not best to have everyone answer every question—a free-flowing discussion is more desirable. But with the opening icebreaker questions, you can go around the circle. Encourage shy people to share, but don't force them.

At your first meeting, let the group members know each session contains a personal study section they can use to continue to engage with the content until the next meeting. While this is optional, it will help them cement the concepts presented during the group study time. Let them know that if they choose to do so, they can watch the video for the next session via streaming. Invite them to bring any questions and insights to your next meeting, especially if they had a breakthrough moment or didn't understand something.

STRUCTURING THE DISCUSSION TIME

You will need to determine how long you want to meet so you can plan your time accordingly. Suggested times for each section have been provided in this study guide, and if you adhere to these times, your group will meet for ninety minutes. If you want to meet for two hours, follow the times given in the right-hand column:

SECTION	90 MINUTES	120 MINUTES
CONNECT (discuss one or more of the opening questions for the session)	10 minutes	15 minutes
WATCH (watch the teaching material together and take notes)	20 minutes	20 minutes
DISCUSS (discuss the study questions you selected ahead of time)	40 minutes	50 minutes
RESPOND (write down key takeaways)	10 minutes	20 minutes
PRAY (pray together and dismiss)	10 minutes	15 minutes

As the group leader, it is up to you to keep track of the time and stay on schedule. You might want to set a timer for each segment so both you and the group members know when your time is up. (There are some good phone apps for timers that play a gentle chime or other upbeat sounds instead of a disruptive noise.)

Don't be concerned if the group members are quiet or slow to share. People are often quiet when they are pulling together their ideas, and this might be a new experience for them. Just ask a question and let it hang in the air until someone shares. You can then say, "Thank you. What about others? What came to you when you watched that portion of the teaching?"

PREPARATION FOR EACH SESSION

As the leader, there are a few things you should do to prepare for each meeting:

- **Read through the session.** This will help you become more familiar with the content and know how to structure the discussion times.
- **Decide how the videos will be used.** Determine whether you want the members to watch the videos ahead of time (via the streaming access code) or together as a group.
- **Decide which questions you want to discuss.** Based on the length of your group discussions, you may not be able to get through all the questions. So look over the questions and choose which ones you definitely want to cover.

- **Be familiar with the questions you want to discuss.** When the group meets, you'll be watching the clock, so make sure you are familiar with the questions that you have selected. In this way, you will ensure that you have the material more deeply in your mind than your group members.
- **Pray for your group.** Pray for your group members and ask God to lead them as they study his Word.

In most cases, there won't be a "right" answer to the question. Answers will vary, especially when the members are being asked to share their personal experiences.

GROUP DYNAMICS

Leading a group through *Habits of the Household* will be rewarding both to you and your group members. But you still may encounter challenges along the way! Discussions can get off track. Group members may not be sensitive to the needs and ideas of others. Some might worry they will be expected to talk about matters that make them feel awkward. Others may express comments that result in disagreements. To help ease this strain on you and the group, consider the following ground rules:

- When someone raises a question or comment that is off the main topic, suggest that you deal with it another time, or, if you feel led to go in that direction, let the group know you will be spending some time discussing it.
- If someone asks a question that you don't know how to answer, admit it and move on. At your discretion, feel free to invite group members to comment on questions that call for personal experience.
- If you find one or two people are dominating the discussion time, direct a few questions to others in the group. Outside the main group time, ask the more dominating members to help you draw out the quieter ones. Work to make them a part of the solution instead of part of the problem.
- When a disagreement occurs, encourage the group members to process the matter in love. Encourage those on opposite sides to restate what they heard the other side say about the matter, and then invite each side to evaluate if that perception is accurate. Lead the group in examining other Scriptures related to the topic and look for common ground.

When any of these issues arise, encourage your group members to follow these words from Scripture: "Love one another" (John 13:34), "If it is possible, as far as it depends on you, live at peace with everyone" (Romans 12:18), "Whatever is true . . . noble . . . right . . . if anything is excellent or praiseworthy—think about such things" (Philippians 4:8), and "Be quick to listen, slow to speak and slow to become angry" (James 1:19). This will make your group time more rewarding and beneficial for everyone who attends.

WEEKEND RETREAT

One additional idea to consider is planning a *Habits of the Household* weekend retreat for couples in your group or church to help them get away from the busyness of life and better connect with the content, with each other, and with God. The goal for the retreat is to create an experience for your group that allows couples to relax and get away from their daily concerns and stresses. The weekend should thus include an element of fun and "down time," where couples can choose how they would like to spend their time together. (It is important to build this into the schedule, as the material covered in the weekend away will impact each couple differently, and so many will welcome the opportunity to step away and relax between sessions.)

Below are schedules for two options: (1) a three-day Friday night to Sunday morning retreat, and (2) a one-day Saturday retreat. The three-day retreat creates unhurried time and space for people to walk through the content, relax, have fun, and discuss ways to incorporate the habits into their daily lives. However, if you find that the majority of the people you are inviting cannot get away for a whole weekend, consider the one-day Saturday option (or some other combination if, for example, most people can attend Friday night and most of the day Saturday). It will take some planning and, likely, some flexibility on your part, but the end result will be worth it.

Sample Three-Day Retreat Schedule
Friday
6:00 PM	Arrive
7:00 PM	Dinner or snacks
8:00 PM	Introduction / icebreaker game
9:00 PM	Session 1: Waking Up to Habits of the Household

Saturday
8:30 AM	Breakfast
9:30 AM	Session 2: Habits for Mealtimes and Family Devotions

10:45 AM	Break and snacks
11:30 AM	Session 3: Habits for Screentime and Formation
1:00 PM	Lunch
2:00 PM	Free time (activities can be organized)
4:00 PM	Snacks
5:00 PM	Session 4: Habits for Using Discipline as Discipleship
6:00 PM	Dinner
8:00 PM	Free time

Sunday

9:00 AM	Breakfast
10:00 AM	Session 5: Habits to Help You Imagine the Future
11:30 AM	Debrief as a group
12:00 PM	Lunch and depart

Sample One-Day Retreat Schedule

Saturday

7:30 AM	Breakfast
8:00 AM	Session 1: Waking Up to Habits of the Household
9:15 AM	Break and snacks
9:30 AM	Session 2: Habits for Mealtimes and Family Devotions
10:30 AM	Break and snacks
11:00 AM	Session 3: Habits for Screentime and Formation
12:00 PM	Lunch
1:00 PM	Session 4: Habits for Using Discipline as Discipleship
2:00 PM	Snacks
2:30 PM	Session 5: Habits to Help You Imagine the Future
3:30 PM	Wrap-up and depart

In closing, thank you for taking the time to lead your group! You are making a difference in your group members' lives and having an impact on their journey as they learn to establish simple but lasting practices that will draw them and their families closer to God.

ABOUT THE AUTHOR

Justin **Whitmel Earley** is a lawyer, author, and speaker from Richmond, Virginia. He graduated from the University of Virginia with a degree in English Literature before spending four years in Shanghai, China, as a missionary. Justin got his law degree from the Georgetown University Law Center and he runs his own business law practice in Richmond, Virginia, at Earley Legal Group. His first book, *The Common Rule–Habits of Purpose for an Age of Distraction,* was published with InterVarsity Press in 2019. His second book, *Habits of the Household–Practicing the Story of God in Everyday Family Rhythms*, released with Zondervan in November of 2021. His third book is *Made for People, Why We Drift into Loneliness and How to Fight for a Life of Friendship.* Justin frequently speaks at businesses and legal events on habits, technology, and mental health and at churches and conferences on habits, spiritual formation, and parenting. He is married to Lauren and has four sons—Whit, Asher, Coulter, and Shep.

ENDNOTES

1. John Ortberg, *The Me I Want to Be* (Grand Rapids, MI: Zondervan, 2009), 51.
2. Will Durant, *The Story of Philosophy* (New York: Simon & Schuster, 1926).
3. Merriam-Webster's Dictionary, s.v. "epiphany," https://www.merriam-webster.com /dictionary/epiphany.
4. Justin Earley, *Habits of the Household* (Grand Rapids, MI: Zondervan, 2021), 25.
5. Earley, *Habits of the Household*, 28.
6. Earley, *Habits of the Household*, 35.
7. Earley, *Habits of the Household*, 196.
8. C. S. Lewis, *The Weight of Glory* (New York: HarperCollins, 2001), 161.
9. Mark Twain, *The Wit and Wisdom of Mark Twain* (New York: Dover Publications, 2013), 44.
10. Tara Parker-Pope, "How to Have Better Family Meals," *New York Times,* https://www .nytimes.com/guides/well/make-most-of-family-table.
11. For the New City Catechism, go to http://sovgraceto.org/wp-content/uploads/2012 /02/Catechism-for-Young-Children.pdf); for the Westminster Shorter Catechism, go to https://www.westminsterconfession.org/resources/confessional-standards/the -westminster-shorter-catechism/.
12. Earley, *Habits of the Household*, 60.
13. Earley, *Habits of the Household*, 60–61.
14. Don Everts, *The Spiritually Vibrant Home* (Downers Grove, IL: InterVarsity Press, 2020), 43–56.
15. See the excellent chapter "Family Is Not First," chapter 4 in Russell Moore, *The Storm-Tossed Family: How the Cross Reshapes the Home* (Nashville: Broadman and Holman, 2018)
16. Genesis 12:2: "I will make you into a great nation, and I will bless you; I will make your name great, and you will be a blessing."
17. Earley, *Habits of the Household*, 62.
18. Tony Reinke, *12 Ways Your Phone Is Changing You* (Wheaton, IL: Crossway, 2017), cited at https://www.crossway.org/articles/12-notable-quotes-from-12-ways-your-phone-is -changing-you/.
19. Robert Mulholland, Jr., *Invitation to a Journey: A Roadmap for Spiritual Formation* (Downers Grove, IL: InterVarsity Press, 2016), 28.

20. Jonathan Haidt, "The Dangerous Experiment on Teen Girls," *The Atlantic,* November 21, 2021, https://www.theatlantic.com/ideas/archive/2021/11/facebooks-dangerous -experiment-teen-girls/620767/.

21. Cited in Jonathan Haidt, "The Dangerous Experiment on Teen Girls."

22. Earley, *Habits of the Household,* 95–96.

23. Edward Luker, "Are Video Games, Screens Another Addiction?" Mayo Clinic Health System, July 1, 2022, https://www.mayoclinichealthsystem.org/hometown-health /speaking-of-health/are-video-games-and-screens-another-addiction.

24. Earley, *Habits of the Household,* 96–97.

25. Earley, *Habits of the Household,* 98.

26. Part of my background for the idea of Christian habits reenchanting a disenchanted world is Charles Taylor's argument that a key feature of our "secular age" is living within a world that cannot see beyond the material. For more on this, see his work *A Secular Age* (Cambridge, MA: Belknap, 2007), or James K. A. Smith's helpful primer *How (Not) to Be Secular: Reading Charles Taylor* (Grand Rapids, MI: Eerdmans, 2014). Mike Cosper also expounds on these themes in *Recapturing the Wonder: Transcendent Faith in a Disenchanted World* (Downers Grove, IL: InterVarsity Press, 2017). The common theme is how all of our cultural assumptions run against the reality of the divine, which means our default cultural mood actively dims our spiritual imagination. In such a moment, what better inheritance can we give our children than a pattern of habits that helps them be aware from a young age that the world is enchanted with the presence of God?

27. Earley, *Habits of the Household,* 164–165.

28. Earley, *Habits of the Household,* 165–166.

29. Earley, *Habits of the Household,* 167–168.

30. Earley, *Habits of the Household,* 169.

31. Henry Cloud, *Necessary Endings* (New York: HarperCollins, 2011), 21.

32. Amy Carmichael, *That Way and No Other* (New York: Plough Publishing House, 2020).

33. Earley, *Habits of the Household,* 72.

34. Earley, *Habits of the Household,* 73.

35. Earley, *Habits of the Household,* 78.

36. Earley, *Habits of the Household,* 187–188.

37. T. S. Eliot, "East Coker," *Four Quartets* (London: Faber and Faber, 1940).

38. Elisabeth Elliot, *Discipline: The Glad Surrender* (Baker, 2006), 126.

39. Earley, *Habits of the Household,* 136–137.

40. Earley, *Habits of the Household,* 142.

41. Earley, *Habits of the Household,* 152.

42. Earley, *Habits of the Household,* 159.

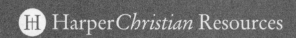

ALSO AVAILABLE

Available now at your favorite bookstore or streaming video on
StudyGateway.com.

ALSO AVAILABLE

Available now at your favorite bookstore or streaming video on
StudyGateway.com.

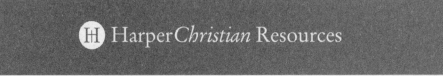